Decorating

IDEA BOOK

Decorating
IDEA BOOK

HEATHER PAPER

The Taunton Press

To Tucker, Murphy, and Dickens

Text © 2005 by The Taunton Press, Inc.
Illustrations © 2005 by The Taunton Press, Inc.

T The Taunton Press
Inspiration for hands-on living®
The Taunton Press, Inc., 63 South Main Street, PO Box 5506, Newtown, CT 06470-5506
e-mail: tp@taunton.com

Editor: Jennifer Matlack
Interior design and layout: Laura Lind Design
Illustrator: Christine Erikson
Cover photographers: Front cover: (top, left & right) Photos © Mark Samu; (bottom left) Photo © Jessie Walker;
(bottom right) Photo © Eric Roth. Front flap: (top) Photo © Brian Vanden Brink, Photographer 2005; (center)
Photo © Jessie Walker; (bottom) Photo © Eric Roth.
Back cover: (top & bottom left) Photos © Eric Roth; (center) Photo © Tim Street-Porter; (bottom right)
Photo © Brian Vanden Brink, Photographer 2005. Back flap: Photo © www.davidduncanlivingston.com.

Library of Congress Cataloging-in-Publication Data
Paper, Heather J.
  Decorating idea book : color, lighting, floors & rugs, walls & windows, storage, accessories / Heather Paper.
      p. cm.
  Includes bibliographical references and index.
  ISBN-13: 978-1-56158-762-9 (alk. paper)
  ISBN-10: 1-56158-762-1 (alk. paper)
  1. Interior decoration--Handbooks, manuals, etc. I. Title.
  NK2115.P278 2005
  747--dc22
                          2005008440

Printed in Singapore
10 9 8 7 6 5 4 3

The following manufacturers/names appearing in *Decorating Idea Book* are trademarks:
Dr. Seuss™, Pez™, Superman™, Thermos®, Ultrasuede™

Acknowledgments

I have to admit, I've never been one of those writers who felt compelled to do a book. I was happy as long as I was writing about decorating in some form or fashion. But when I was asked to write Taunton's *Decorating Idea Book*, it was a dream come true. I just didn't know I'd been dreaming about it.

Even for someone with years of writing experience, the prospect of a book can seem daunting. And I couldn't have done it without the team at Taunton Press. Special thanks go to Carolyn Mandarano, Jen Matlack, Julie Hamilton, Jenny Peters, and Wendi Mijal. They were not only the ultimate pros but also my biggest cheerleaders along the way. Thanks, too, to Maureen Graney, who initially brought me into the project.

I also owe a special thank you to my long-time editor and friend, Shirley Van Zante. Under her tutelage at *Better Homes & Gardens*, I learned how to be a better writer. She taught me how to recognize good decorating ideas and then how to translate them to the reader. There's not a day that goes by that her guidance doesn't still affect me in some way, personally and professionally.

There are countless friends and family members to be thanked for their support, too numerous to mention (and for fear that I might leave someone out). Something as simple as "How's the book going?" would let me know that they were thinking of me. A special thank you, though, goes to Debbie Geiger. She's one of those through-thick-and-thin friends that you feel lucky to have.

Last but not least, I want to thank my husband and best friend, Russ, whose love and support inspire me every day. Without him, I wouldn't be the writer—or the person—that I am today.

Contents

Introduction ▪ 4

Chapter 1
The Comforts of Home ▪ 6

The Big Picture ▪ 8

Sharpening Your Vision ▪ 13

Decorating Decisions ▪ 14

Chapter 2
Color ▪ 16

Picking a Palette ▪ 18

Setting the Mood ▪ 22

Incorporating Color ▪ 44

Chapter 3
Furniture · 56

Sofas · 58

Chairs · 66

Tables · 82

Beds · 104

Desks · 118

Chapter 4
Room Arrangements · 124

The Entry · 126

The Family Room · 132

The Great Room · 138

The Living Room · 144

The Dining Room · 150

The Bedroom · 156

Chapter 5
Window Treatments · 162

Draperies · 164

Blinds and Shades · 176

Shutters · 184

Chapter 6

Wall Coverings · 186

Paint · 188

Wallpaper · 196

Tile · 202

Fabric · 206

The Fifth Wall · 208

Chapter 7

Floor Coverings · 210

Carpet · 212

Hardwoods · 222

Resilient Flooring · 228

Nonresilient Flooring · 234

Chapter 8

Storage Solutions · 242

Chests · 244

Armoires · 248

Entertainment Centers · 250

Dressers and Nightstands · 252

China Cabinets · 254

Sideboards and Buffets · 256

Display Units · 258

Freestanding Storage · 260

Built-Ins · 262

Chapter 9

Lighting · 270

Ambient Lighting · 272

Task Lighting · 280

Accent Lighting · 284

Chapter 10

Decorative Accessories · 288

Wall Art · 290

Collectibles · 298

Mantels · 304

Soft Stuff · 308

Credits · 310

Introduction

I am one of the lucky ones. I managed to "follow my bliss" before it was fashionable. As far back as I can remember, I have been fascinated by decorating. Even during grammar-school days, I would look forward to the falling leaves of autumn, not because I could create piles to jump into, like my brother did. Instead, I used them to build the "walls" of my dream house, the floor plan laid out in my own backyard.

It was a passion that never disappeared, so it was no surprise to anyone that I studied interior design in college. But just as I was about to walk away from those hallowed halls, degree in hand, I had a brainstorm.

Writing was another great interest of mine, so why not combine the two? I did a little "redesigning" of my course load and eventually walked away with a double major in interior design and journalism.

Over the years I've had the pleasure of writing about grand homes and those decorated on a dime. And there's really no difference. Creativity doesn't have a price tag, which you'll find proven—time and time again—within the pages of this book. These pages are filled with information and inspiration, taking you step by step through the decorating process, from finding your personal style to selecting the right accessories.

Decorating is an evolution, a never-ending process. Styles change. Tastes change. Even families change. Through it all, you'll want to keep this book close at hand, guiding you along the way. Even if I hadn't written *Decorating Idea Book* I'd want it on my bookshelves. I'm glad you feel the same way.

The Comforts of Home

There's no disputing the fact that the home has become the center of our universe. It's a safe place to land; after a long day at work, our home is a haven amidst the hustle and bustle of the outside world. It's also a comfortable place to gather with family, proven by the large number of great rooms being incorporated into today's floor plans. Even smaller houses are being remodeled to create more space for relaxing and entertaining.

The "return to home" is also evidenced by the sheer number of families that are once again sitting down at mealtime together. And consider how many families are opting to entertain friends and colleagues. From last-minute potlucks to elegant dinner parties, sharing a home-cooked meal is still one of the best ways to a man's (or woman's) heart.

And, while you're at it, why not make it dinner and a movie? Today's big-screen televisions, theatre-style seating, and the quick release of even the latest films give "home movies" an entirely new meaning.

The comforts of home are affecting our work lives as well. Now more than ever, men and women are choosing to be self-employed, working from home offices. Others are opting to telecommute, ridding themselves of the stress of daily back-and-forth traffic. More women, too, are electing to take on the role of full-time moms, spending the majority of the day in the sanctity of their own households. Some are even taking that concept a step further, preferring to home school their children— at least, during those early, formative years.

◄ IN THIS LIVING ROOM, red upholstered seating pieces add spice to an otherwise subdued color scheme. The coffee table serves double duty: The light and dark tones echo those of the nearby fireplace while storage drawers provide a place for magazines, remote controls, and other small items.

THE BIG PICTURE

Creating comfortable living quarters is more than a matter of shopping for a new piece of furniture, however. Whether you're starting from scratch or simply doing a little redecorating, it's important to first take a look at the big picture. Determine whether your family members live formally or if they are more laid back. Take a look, too, at what colors and styles you like most. Last, but not least, be sure to figure kids and pets into the equation.

Personal Style

The way that you like to live—and, let's face it, most of us fall into the casual category—will have a strong influence on the way you

▲ SLIPCOVERS LIKE THE ONES SEEN HERE can be the perfect solution for active families; when they get soiled, they can simply be thrown into the washing machine. Plus, neutral hues like these leave the possibilities wide open for accent colors like the reds and blues in this room.

◄ THERE'S NO RULE THAT A FORMAL DINING ROOM has to be, well, formal. This black-painted, picnic-style table teams up with simple aluminum chairs to create a one-of-a-kind look that is well suited to the owners' casual lifestyle.

▲ SERVING THE MAIN SEATING GROUP in this living room is an ottoman with an ingenious design. The upholstered top offers put-your-feet-up comfort yet is firm enough to hold a tray of snacks. Meanwhile, a wooden surface below echoes the round shape, providing a convenient place for books.

◄ TRADITIONAL ELEGANCE NEED NOT BE STIFF
or overly fussy. Here, a cream and gold wallpaper establishes a quiet color scheme. In turn, uncomplicated furnishings, such as the corner chair, fringed ottoman, and floor-length window treatment carry out the pattern's subdued hues.

▼ MODERN CLASSICS TAKE CENTER STAGE in this living room. An understated backdrop, including window treatments that blend into the wall and a fireplace surround that's nothing less than discreet, allows the attention to be placed squarely on the sculptural furnishings.

decorate your home. So, too, will your preferences in terms of furniture styles. Are you most relaxed in a traditional setting, complete with camelback sofas and wing chairs? Or are you at the opposite end of the spectrum, preferring sleek contemporary styles? If you're unsure, try this simple exercise: Thumb through this book, looking for rooms that you find appealing; there will be some common decorating threads among them that will give you a sense of where to start. You may even find that you like elements of several different styles, putting you in the eclectic category—one of the best ways to put your personal stamp on a room.

Use a traditional four-poster bed here and a contemporary Le Corbusier chaise there. As long as the disparate styles all have clean, classic forms, they'll work together beautifully.

Color Cues

Purely personal, too, is your choice of a color palette. Like specific furniture styles, colors can speak volumes about your individual tastes. For instance, a bedroom done in subdued shades of beige is by no means an indication of the owner's bland personality. Rather, it speaks to the need for a calming influence at the end of the day.

 OPPOSITES ATTRACT, AND IT'S MOST EVIDENT when furnishings—and accent colors—are minimal. A modern Le Corbusier chaise is right at home with a country-style pine settee. Strengthening the contrasting pieces, a black rug echoes the drama of the chaise while the pine floor repeats the settee's wood tone.

On the other hand, a dining room wrapped in salsa red offers a clue that the home-owner has a distinct, dramatic flair.

When it comes to color, some people are unsure about which ones to choose—and how much to use. A reliable gauge is as close as your own closet. Are you a jeans-and-T-shirt type? If so, navy blue may be one of the colors you're most comfortable with. Or take the color cue even more literally: Choose a blue denim sofa for your family room and accent it with throw pillows in bright T-shirt shades. Likewise, if your closet is brimming with soft, sherbet colors, you'll no doubt be most relaxed in rooms decorated in the same tones.

Real-Life Living

The most beautiful decorating scheme will fall flat if it's not designed with specific family members in mind. The natural wear and tear that comes from children at play, for instance, has to be considered when selecting new fur-nishings. Tough-as-nails chenille fabrics are obviously a better choice than delicate silks. And medium to dark colors are always more family friendly than stark whites. (You can imagine what spilled grape juice would do to the latter!) Even in the category of floor cov-erings there are some options that are better than others. Sisal rugs, for example, may be good looking but are hard on the knees of a little one just learning to crawl. And carpets

▶ ALTHOUGH A PASTEL PALETTE WASHES OVER THIS LIVING ROOM, there's nothing timid about it. The yellow walls and warm-hued furnishings fill the space with brightness. The room's white trim also plays an important role: It provides visual relief from the profusion of color.

with built-in stain resistance are much easier to clean, whether you're dealing with the kids' tracked-in dirt or a pet's "accident." On the other hand, single adults and empty nesters or anyone else in a kid-free environment have more expanded options. They can feel perfectly comfortable surrounding themselves with luxurious linen fabrics and sophisticated marble floors, not to mention all kinds of fine collectibles.

SHARPENING YOUR VISION

Once you have the big picture of your room squarely in sight—including major pieces of furniture and color choices—it's time to con-

centrate on individual elements. Do this by simply starting from the outside of the room and working in. Using the patterns and colors in your upholstered pieces as inspiration, select window and wall coverings that will provide the best surround for your scheme. If you want the pieces of furniture to stand out, take an "art gallery" approach and treat the windows and walls in a subdued way, which doesn't necessarily mean white. For example, paint the walls a sophisticated taupe, then dress the windows in simple Roman shades that match the wall color. Conversely, you might opt to make the backdrop the shining star of the show by drench-

▲ INSPIRATION CAN COME FROM
ANYWHERE. In this horse barn-
turned-home, built-in color cues
inspired the room schemes: The
stained glass windows, in shades
of purple and red, were part of
the original building.

ing it in a bold hue taken from a predominant pattern in the room.

Once window and wall coverings are
determined, shift your focus downward to
the floor. Whatever you choose for this large
expanse of space can have a tremendous
effect on the overall outcome. Once you've
made all of your careful choices, make sure
that they're showcased properly with the
right lighting.

As you work your way through the decorating process, whether you're working on
one room or an entire house, take time to
enjoy the experience. That's especially true
once you get down to the finishing touches.
More than anything else, accessories speak
to others of your tastes, your travels, your
personal experiences, and your family.

DECORATING DECISIONS

It's comforting to know that there are no
right or wrong approaches to decorating.
But with today's easy access to the information highway, the number of options can be
intimidating. Keep in mind that it all comes
down to individual style. And remember that
there are guidelines to help along the way.

In the pages that follow, you'll find an
impressive collection of photos that convey a
wealth of decorating ideas. Let them take
you through the process, then translate them
to your own personal tastes. You'll undoubtedly end up with a room that's as pretty as it
is practical, as calming as it is comfortable. In
other words, you can have it all.

► THE OWNER'S LOVE FOR THE SEA is evident by the nautical-inspired accessories throughout this home office. The crowning touch in terms of personal style, however, is the "Sea Gypsy" verse that's been painted right onto the wall; the same technique can be translated to reflect any personal interest.

▼ WITH A PAIR OF HIS-AND-HER WING CHAIRS FLANKING A LOVESEAT, this living area is all about relaxation. The red seating pieces are outfitted with plump throw pillows and wrap-up-in quilts that reflect the primary hue while adding an extra element of comfort.

Color

Color is a constant influence in our everyday lives. Just think of the blinking reds and greens of traffic signals that tell us when to stop and go. Or the warm yellow sun that beats down, causing us to shed our layers. It's no surprise, then, that color is equally influential in the home.

Traditionally, certain colors have been designated for specific spaces—pink or blue in the nursery, hunter green in the library, and pure white in the master bath. But in this age of eclectic decorating, anything goes, including color. Today, it's not unusual to see bright hues in a baby's room. And libraries are no longer quite so dark and masculine. Even master baths are now commonly splashed with bold color.

The bottom line is that the colors you use in your decorating scheme should readily reflect your personality, be it softly feminine, solidly traditional, or quietly contemporary. That way, you'll give your guests a little insight into who you are each time they step through the front door. More important, though, when you come home at the end of the day, you'll always feel comfortable.

◄ THE PERIWINKLE BLUE HUES that prevail in this bedroom create a restful and relaxing atmosphere. Neutral white surfaces and warm wood elements provide a balance, though, because too much of this cool color would make the space seem cold rather than comfortable.

Picking a Palette

PICK UP A STACK OF PAINT CHIPS and you'll understand why choosing a palette can seem daunting: There are limitless colors available. To make the decision process less difficult, begin by looking for a few clues. We all have a favorite color so start by simply considering the various tints and shades within that color family. Also think about the room and how it will be used. Is it a living area where you'll entertain often? If so, consider neutral hues that will make most guests comfortable. For a home office opt for lively colors instead of hues that are too sedate, or else you might end up napping instead of working. The biggest clue of all, however, is your wardrobe. Take a look at the colors you wear each day. Chances are, if you're comfortable wearing them, you'll be comfortable living with them, too.

▲ EACH ROOM CAN HAVE A COLOR personality all its own. This living room, with pale yellow walls, has a sunny disposition. Meanwhile, the adjacent dining room—decked out in a brilliant red—makes a dramatic impression. Crisp white trim links the two spaces together.

◀ THIS COLOR SCHEME covers the gamut of cool hues, from the blue seating pieces to green window treatments to rich purple-painted walls to an area rug that incorporates them all. The effect is whimsical but, at the same time, completely soothing.

A Smooth Blend

IN THE PROCESS OF DECORATING A ROOM, it's easy to spend too many hours trying to match colors. In fact, that's not necessary, or in many cases, even desirable. It's more important that colors blend. For example, if you have two or three blues within a room, they'll be right at home together if they're of similar tones and intensities.

If you're unsure whether your colors will work together, try this simple test: Gather the colors together, step back, and look at them through squinted eyes. If they seem to become a single shade, then you have a beautiful blend of colors.

▲ THIS LIVING ROOM FOLLOWS A TRIED-AND-TRUE 60/30/10 FORMULA, using patterns that have colors in common. The predominant geometric print appears on the sofa, armchairs, and curtains, while a paisley rug—secondary to the scheme—softens the look. A stylized floral print on the dining chairs and throw pillows provides a welcome accent.

▲ NO MATTER HOW COMFORTABLE it may be, this gray sofa would have been drab in another setting. Here, though, the cool color is warmed up considerably with lemon yellow walls and throw pillows in the same bright hue.

► AS THE HEART OF THE HOME, the kitchen should provide a sense of warmth. To keep this red one from heating up too much, the ceiling and stair balusters are painted white as are the walls of the adjacent room. Even the white enamelware adds a cool touch.

ELEMENTS OF DESIGN

Harmony

IN ANY SUCCESSFUL SCHEME, there has to be some kind of unifying theme that runs through the room, blending everything together. That's where harmony comes in. Of all design principals, it's perhaps the most vital. Without it, a room lacks cohesiveness.

Achieving harmony is not as difficult as it may sound. For starters, furniture should be of the right scale. Squat seating pieces aren't particularly appropriate for spaces with high, soaring ceilings. And oversize armoires aren't a good fit for homes that have standard-height rooms. Likewise, fabrics should be a good match for their frames. For example, chenille is perfectly appropriate for overstuffed sofas but out of place on delicate Louis XVI chairs.

Color, though, is where harmony is at its most critical. It's imperative that there be at least one or two common threads of color. You can use multiple patterns within a room as long as you can connect them somehow. Maybe they all have an element of red or slightly varied shades of blue. It's no different, really, than putting together a fashionable ensemble.

▲ USING ONLY WARM OR COOL hues in a room makes it easier to create a harmonious scheme. The color palette in this library covers the entire warm range, from the yellow table to the orange chair to the ruby red bookshelves.

Setting the Mood

THERE'S LITTLE DOUBT THAT COLOR IS EMOTIONAL. Why else would we be "green with envy" or "feeling blue"? Every color of the rainbow conveys a mood. By playing up specific shades, you'll translate those feelings to your room, too.

From a decorating point of view, red is a passionate, powerful hue because it stimulates everything, including the appetite. That's why it's a good choice for a dining room. Blue, on the other hand, is restful, making it appropriate for the bedroom. Yellow is cheery, green is refreshing, and purple—even today—has a regal feeling. Before you wrap a room in color, though, consider the feeling it evokes. You want to be sure that the mood you create is appropriate to the space.

▲ BLUE PROVIDES a sense of soothing serenity in the bedroom. This space plays off the tints and shades of the wallpaper pattern, ranging from the pale blue bed trim to the deep blue easy chair. The white bed linens keep things light and airy.

▶ WRAPPING A ROOM IN RED is a sure-fire way to add warmth. This library uses the solid hue on the sofa, built-in bookshelves, and high-gloss trim. There's plenty of pattern to balance it, though, in the curtains and pillows, upholstered armchairs, and even a fabric-covered wall panel.

▲ CORAL AND WHITE CABANA STRIPES on slipcovered seating pieces and matching curtains conjure up a beach-like atmosphere in this living area. Meanwhile, the rest of the room's furnishings are minimal, further carrying out the feeling of a peaceful retreat.

EXCITING

▲ THERE'S NOTHING STUFFY ABOUT THIS ROOM, thanks to cool green contemporary hues. Set on either side of the fireplace, a pair of plaid chaises adds visual energy, complemented by a bench that brings the lemony lime curtain color to the center of the room.

◄ OPPOSITE THE PLAID CHAISES, solid-color seating pieces create a comfortable seating group. But don't confuse solid with sedate. A sofa in a neutral hue is punctuated with pillows in vibrant colors. The real excitement, though, comes from two slipper chairs, covered in a daring fuchsia.

▼ HERE, RICH RED HUES start at the floor and run up to the ceiling. To keep the color from being overpowering, it's punctuated with crisp white trim. But the preeminent regal feeling comes from the accent hue—the gold of the curtains, the ceiling, and the mirror.

Try a New Hue

READY TO TAKE THE PLUNGE and saturate a room in an exciting new hue? Before committing to expensive upholstery or fixtures, try living with it in small doses first. Decorative pillows and throws can provide good clues in the living room while a new tablecloth can serve the same purpose in a dining room or an eat-in kitchen. In a bedroom, the same can be accomplished with a new set of sheets. The bottom line: Start slowly and work up to the level of color that you're comfortable with.

▲ THIS BEDROOM has enough excitement to make things interesting but not so much that it causes distraction. Touches of blue anchor the white bed and flank the sheer curtains, while red accents add a refreshing hint of warm color.

▲ A TILE-TOP TABLE is backed by a deep blue wall in this outdoor dining area, evoking the hues of the Caribbean Sea. The addition of white accents in the tabletop and chairs, as well as the white-painted wood floor, gives the space a tranquil yet refreshing feeling.

Turn Up the Temperature

DO YOU HAVE A NORTH-FACING ROOM that seems to have a chill even during summer? Or one with minimal windows, restricting the amount of sunlight that it gets? Without touching the thermometer, you can raise the temperature of a room with color. Just look at the warm side of the color palette and use it to your advantage. Consider yellow, for instance. In its most vibrant form, it can add visual warmth to even the coolest space.

To take the concept a step further, consider red. Not only does this hue have the ability to add heat but it provides plenty of drama, too. Likewise, the orange hue that you associate with the fruit is only one of the tints and shades you can use in a room. In pale cantaloupe colors and cinnamon shades, it adds an element of excitement. And in the form of peach or apricot, this color is perfectly suited for a living area. The latter two hues, "cosmetic colors" naturally complement skin tones, adding a warm glow to everyone in the room.

▲ IT'S COMMON KNOWLEDGE that a large room can be difficult to heat, even with a massive stone fireplace. This space accomplishes it quite simply with color. Sunny yellows cover the walls and upholstered seating pieces, visually warming the room.

▲ BRILLIANT HUES CAN TRANSFORM VICTORIAN FURNITURE into something fresh. The wooden frames of these seating pieces keep them true to their original vintage while the vibrant upholstery patterns bring them into the contemporary realm. It's eclectic decorating at its best.

▲ THIS BEDROOM COMBINES COOL COLORS in a fresh way. A simple green and white striped wallpaper provides the backdrop, inspiring the green slipper chair, pillows, and accessories. The surprise addition, though, is the lavender hue. It makes a strong showing but isn't overwhelming.

▲ USING TINTS AND SHADES of a single hue creates a cohesive color scheme. A dark purple sofa anchors this room. The ottoman, central to the seating pieces, is in a slightly lighter shade while a pale lavender armchair quietly blends into the backdrop.

◄ IT DOESN'T TAKE MUCH COLOR to keep a white room from appearing too cold. This one doesn't need anything more than an aqua throw rug in front of the fireplace, the aged copper roof on a decorative birdhouse, and the warmth of the wood floor.

Cooling Off

JUST AS WARM COLORS CAN RAISE THE TEMPERATURE OF A ROOM, **cool hues can drop it by a few degrees.** Think of a solarium, surrounded with windows, that's almost too warm to appreciate. Or maybe a second-floor office or attic bedroom where the heat consistently rises.

In these cases and others like it, cool colors can come to the rescue, especially those on the lighter side. In the blue family, consider the color of the sky. Or look toward the colors of the Caribbean—in their palest form at the water's edge and gradually getting darker as you move farther out.

To take another cue from Mother Nature, consider assorted greens, as well. Leafy greens have springtime-fresh appeal, while celery shades are more subtle. In all cases, though, couple the cool colors with at least a touch of icy white; it not only will give you a crisp finish but will also provide more chill to the space.

▶ A WARM WOOD CEILING AND FLOOR with sunshine streaming through multiple windows could make this bathroom seem too warm. But liberal amounts of cool greens and blues keep the visual temperature at a comfortable level.

▶ THIS LIVING ROOM IS WRAPPED in a dusty blue, a hue inspired by the water and sky just outside the windows, blurring the boundaries between outdoors and in. Furnishings in a variety of warm earth tones keep the cool space from turning cold.

▲ PALE BLUE HUES SURROUND THE ENTRANCE to this master bath, creating the feeling of a soothing spa. The space beyond delivers, too, outfitted with cool white tile warmed up just slightly by the lavender-pink walls and the warm wood trim.

▶ A MIX OF SOLIDS, PRINTS, AND STRIPES is important to any well-designed room. It's easier to combine them, though, if you stick to one color. Green is the common denominator here, showing up in a variety of patterns. The solid-color wall provides the needed balance.

ROMANTIC

▲ A ROMANTIC AMBIENCE can start right at the front door, proven by this skirted table topped with lighting that casts a soft glow. The dining room beyond—with its pastel floral wall covering—further evokes a soft mood.

▶ DELICATE COLORS AND TRADITIONAL FURNITURE add up to a strong sense of romance in this living room. The pale green of the walls and the armchair is completely peaceful, whereas the peach damask sofa and fireside ottoman balance things with just the right touch of warmth.

◀ TO KEEP THE BLUE AND WHITE FLORAL PATTERN from overwhelming this bedroom, white bed linens provide a visual resting place. Set against the delicate pattern, the four-poster gets more emphasis, too, taking on an almost sculptural look.

The New Neutrals

IT USED TO BE THAT BLACK, WHITE, AND BEIGE were the three basic neutral hues. Their inherent beauty was that they went with everything. Then camel, taupe, and gray provided more variations on the theme. Today, however, the "new neutrals" have a completely new definition: They are colors that simply complement most of the others in the spectrum.

The right shade is important, though. A buttery yellow goes with just about everything, but a neon yellow or more somber shade doesn't have the same effect. And the same goes for green. Spring greens or something closer to sage are your best options; think of how the first greens of spring complement every imaginable flower or how a dusty, herbal shade has chameleon qualities. Even peach has made its way into the category of new neutrals.

▲ JUST LOOK AT A FLOWER STEM and you'll realize that every color goes well with green. In fact, many of today's new neutrals come directly from nature, including pale yellow, peach, and the sage green of these bedspreads that complements every other color in the room.

▲ THE YELLOW THAT WRAPS THIS ROOM in the window and wall treatments qualifies as one of today's new neutrals. Because the shade is a pale mustard, and not too bright or dull, it remains quietly in the background, allowing the furnishings to take center stage.

◄ ENVELOPED IN A SUNNY YELLOW COLOR that's repeated in accessories as well as in the entryway wallpaper, this room exudes a warm country charm. A surprise focal point is in the red and white checked curtains, a design element that usually blends quietly into the background.

▼ A SOFT-COLORED FLORAL SOFA and two matching chairs give this room a feminine flair. The area rug echoes the hues, but most of the remaining furnishings—as well as the walls—are in solid colors, allowing the two primary patterns to take the spotlight.

▲ CANOPIES, LIKE THE ONE THAT FRAMES THIS POSTER BED, are often equated with romantic rooms, especially when fashioned out of soft floral fabrics. Here, the pattern has been translated onto the walls, too: Hand-painted floral swags seemingly hang from the ceiling's edge, eventually fading into a mottled blue hue.

◀ FRENCH FURNISHINGS lend themselves to romance. Here, pale lavender hues throughout the bedroom are inspired by the herb that the country is famous for. Because the colors are all equal in their intensity, everything is on the same quiet level.

▲ WITH WHITE UPHOLSTERED PIECES—even a white cloth skirting the end table—this room is both understated and sophisticated. The pale yellow of the walls is considered a neutral shade because it complements so many colors of the spectrum.

► COLOR CAN COME from sources other than fabric or paint. Here, camel-colored sofas and warm beige walls are only the beginning of the story. Just as important to the subdued scheme are natural elements such as the sisal rug and the limestone and wrought-iron coffee table.

◄ DEPENDING ON HOW DARK OR LIGHT its shade is, beige can be either a cool or warm color. The beige fabrics in this office are on the cool side, but they are warmed up with wood surfaces—the coffee table, desk, and paneling.

▼ DRESSED IN ASSORTED SHADES of cream and white, this bedroom counts on a variety of textures to keep things interesting, including the wood frame of the chair, the sisal area rug, and the bed's nailhead trim, frequently found on upholstered furniture.

Texture

WHILE TEXTURE MAY NOT BE AS GLAMOROUS as color or pattern, it is essential to any room. Nowhere, though, is it more important than in a room decked out in entirely neutral hues.

Think about a room with seating pieces covered in white cotton fabrics and curtains made of the same material. Picture a wooden coffee table and hardwood floor with similarly smooth surfaces. Undoubtedly, this room could be considered well designed, but without texture, it falls flat.

Now think about that same room, but replace the white cotton on the seating pieces with a highly textured linen. Replace the window curtains with a sheer stripe and add a craggy, limestone top to the coffee table. Finally, cover the hardwood floor with an area rug with a nubby texture such as sisal. Your reward is a room rich in design—and diversity.

▲ IN THIS LIVING ROOM, the key to success is in the mix. While the color palette takes a subtle, slightly varied approach, assorted textures—from the smooth wood tabletop to the coarse sisal rug—combine to keep things interesting.

▲ THIS GREAT ROOM IS DECORATED in variations of the neutral hues, from creamy whites to warm browns, allowing the people who fill the space to provide the color. The large windows and floral arrangement on the table bring in the natural colors of the outdoors.

◄ A FAUX BOIS (French for "false wood") fabric pattern is the mainstay of this cool color scheme. It's supported by a variety of neutral partners, ranging from the white linens to the bronze lamp base. The wooden bedside table adds a touch of warmth to the room.

WHIMSICAL

▶ IT'S SIMPLE TO TAKE A ROOM from functional to fun. This rustic bedroom gets its wit from a pair of bedspreads and a small rug—that's all. By keeping the backdrop low key, like these log cabin walls and hardwood flooring, whimsical pieces will command more attention.

▼ IN THIS PLAY SPACE, navy blue emphasizes the architecture of one wall, while an oversize chair in the same shade provides some balance. The real fun, though, comes from the hopscotch rug, diamond-adorned storage cabinets, and a red chair with a Dr. Seuss™-like shape.

▲ A FUN-FILLED FABRIC sets the tone in this bedroom. The predominant red, yellow, and blue hues reappears on the bed pillows while a soft "neutral" green complements the primary scheme, and offers the eye a visual resting place. A chandelier adds to the fanciful theme.

► INSPIRED BY THE ARTWORK above the fireplace, this color scheme starts with black and white sofas and is anchored by a cherry red rug. From there, every color in the rainbow shows up. What makes the room work is that each hue is just as vibrant as the rug.

▼ THE SAME COLORS that take on a childlike quality in one room can be perfectly suitable for adults in another. In this case, a softer shade of purple and more sophisticated patterns are responsible for the change of mood.

► PROMPTED BY THE WHIMSICAL BED LINENS, cool colors reach new levels in this bedroom. On the wall, lavender climbs to the ceiling in thin stripes; on the floor, periwinkle takes the form of a diamond pattern. Even a blue window topper does its part to carry out the scheme.

Linking Rooms with Color

Today's open floor plans—kitchens to family rooms and formal living to dining rooms—make it more important than ever to link one room to another with color.

So how do you give each room its own personality and still keep things cohesive? Repetition is key, but not in a literal sense. For instance, if you paint your kitchen cabinets a spicy salsa red, that doesn't mean that you should do the same to the bookcases in the adjacent family room. Instead, reuse the red hue in a similar amount but in a different way. Select a red sofa and matching chairs or dress the bay window in a hot red.

The same theory also works for side-by-side living and dining rooms. In the dining room, paint the dado, the portion of the wall under the chair rail, in a rich mocha color; then repeat the color on a tall, vertical wall in the living room—the fireplace wall, for instance. The possibilities are endless.

▲ IN ADJACENT ROOMS, blue and white schemes are anchored by tile floors in slate blue hues. Each area gets an extra dose of the color, too, but in different ways. The kitchen echoes it on the walls, while the sun room repeats it in the seat cushions.

Incorporating Color

THERE'S NO END TO THE VARIETY OF WAYS that color can be incorporated into a room. It just depends on how much color you're comfortable with. You may, for instance, still be at the point of taking baby steps, only wanting a very small dose. And that's just fine since many a sophisticated scheme is made up of subtle neutrals, punctuated only by colorful accessories here and there. To go to the next level, however, drench the walls, the ceiling, and even the floor in color. If you use paint, it's easy to cover up if you're not satisfied the first time. If you're truly courageous with color, then bring it into a room with an assortment of wallpaper and furniture fabrics. You'll know you've graduated into the world of color when you cover the walls in lemon yellow or order your first lipstick red sofa.

▼ A CHOCOLATE BROWN AND POWDER BLUE color scheme draws the eye in this bedroom. The bed's shapely style also demands attention, which it achieves by being set in a recessed niche—painted the same powder blue hue—and illuminated with twin wall-hung reading lamps on either side.

WITH A PALE BACKDROP and hardwood floors, this dining room is free to incorporate color at every turn. The two-tone table, upholstered chair cushions, plaid Roman shades, and whimsical rug add vibrant punches of color to this space.

A TONE-ON-TONE COLOR SCHEME can go from low-key to lackluster without a few punches of color here and there. All that's needed in this room are hardcover books, with their varied jackets, and a prominently placed work of art.

WITH A PIECE OF FURNITURE as powerful as this red leather sectional, it's important to allow it to take the spotlight. Case in point: The yellow leather chairs opposite the sofa aren't quiet in their own right but do blend quietly into a backdrop of the same hue.

FURNITURE AND ACCESSORIES

▲ IN THIS INTIMATE SEATING GROUP, color and shape are equally important. The sofa, for instance, is upholstered in a simple white, but bright red welting accentuates its tailored form. Meanwhile, the mere placement of the two armless chairs makes their silhouettes almost sculptural.

◄ PASTELS ARE NOT RESTRICTED to the nursery. Here, a striped headboard provides the starting point, its mostly pink hues complemented by the soft blue walls. The cool hue makes its way onto the bed linens, too, which bring more geometric shapes into the mix.

▼ EACH AREA IN THIS GREAT ROOM is anchored by a color— a red table and stools in the casual dining area, blue tile at the eating counter, and an aqua sofa in the conversation group. The predominant colors overlap, though, making the room work well as a whole.

▶ SOME COLORS JUST GO TOGETHER NATURALLY, like red, white, and blue. Here, a navy hue covers the floor and comforter, and a slightly paler shade dresses the window. The red-painted bed adds warmth while the white wall strikes an overall balance.

Mixing Patterns

WHEN MIXING PATTERNS IN A ROOM, just remember that it's as easy as one, two, three. First, if you're a beginner, stick to three basic prints. You'll want a large-scale pattern for big pieces such as the sofa, a medium-scale that will work on easy chairs and ottomans, and a mini-print appropriate for pillows and other small items. Keep in mind that all three patterns should have common denominator colors, too. That is, if blue and yellow are your key colors, make sure that all three patterns incorporate similar shades of each. If you're unsure how to go about it, take advantage of today's wealth of premixed fabric collections. Manufacturers have made sure that you can't go wrong.

Once you've decided on your three patterns, consider how they will be used in the room. To keep things balanced, it's best to use each pattern three times—once in a major way, again on something smaller, and then a third time as an accent somewhere. For example, you might use your largest-scale pattern once on the sofa, once on a table skirt, and finally on a decorative pillow. Go through the same thought process for all three patterns. Before long, you'll be master of the mix.

▲ THIS PROFUSION OF PATTERN blends beautifully, thanks to the well-coordinated color palette; there are strong common threads of red, yellow, and blue running throughout. Key to the room's success are solid-color accessories in the same hues to provide a resting place for the eye.

▲ THESE CORAL-COLORED SEATING PIECES are anchored by a rug that incorporates the same warm palette. Meanwhile, bright yellow walls accentuate the coral tones, in the furniture as well as in the lampshades, and create an uplifting atmosphere.

◄ INSPIRED BY THE ARTWORK at the far end of the room, this space features a storage piece that replicates its shapes and colors. Even the table repeats the predominant rectangular form. The red chairs add a splash of vibrant color and soften the scheme with a few curves.

▲ THIS SOFA'S FLORAL MOTIF inspired the room's color scheme. The predominant yellow hue appears on the chairs and the walls, but these elements co-exist quietly, allowing the sofa to stand out. Meanwhile, the hardwood floor, with its reddish tone, adds more warmth to the room.

▲ THE BLUE HUE above the crisp white wainscoting in this room provides a dramatic backdrop for treasured works of art. Because the color doesn't reach all the way to the ceiling, it gives the space a more intimate feeling.

▲ A LIVELY LEAFY GREEN wraps this home office. By painting everything the same color—the walls, the trim, even the window mullions—other furnishings command attention, including the sculptural desk, a tailored window treatment, and the gentle curves of the terra-cotta-colored chair.

TRICKS OF THE TRADE

Strokes of Genius

TOO OFTEN, A ROOM'S PAINT COLOR IS CHOSEN from a 1-in.-wide paint chip and the results are disappointing. There is a solution, though. Once you've narrowed your choices to two or three, buy a small amount of each color. Then, go to your local do-it-yourself center and purchase pieces of foam core approximately 2 ft. square for each one. Paint each piece of foam core one of the colors, then prop them all against one wall of the room and study them at different times of the day. Move the pieces from wall to wall, as light can affect each one differently.

▲ THANKS TO THEIR HIGHLY TEXTURED APPEARANCE, these wine-colored walls are even more striking. The texture provides an appealing contrast, too—in both color and finish—for the sleek fireplace as well as for the smooth wood floors.

▼ A DEEP CRIMSON COLOR adds drama to a room, not to mention heat. Here, red and white-striped curtains provide visual relief for the solid hue, as does the crisp white ceiling and molding. The patterned carpet also plays a role in balancing its intensity.

◄ WALLS DECKED OUT IN FLORAL PATTERNS can be spectacular, more so if they're kept in check with generous amounts of solid color. White-painted woodwork does its part here to offset the pattern, as do the seating pieces, all in the same soft coral color.

▲ WHEN USING A SOLID COLOR on a large surface like a wall, it's important to use it sparingly throughout the rest of the space. Otherwise, it loses its importance. Here, the wall's periwinkle color briefly reappears on plaid Roman shades and in an upholstered chair and area rug.

QUICK FIX

Seasonal Color

IF YOU ENJOY THE CHANGE OF SEASONS, bring it inside with a little quick-change artistry. Take a look at your window treatment, for instance. Do you have a combination of draperies and sheers? During the warm summer months, pare down by removing the draperies and letting the sheers stand alone. Or if you have curtains with a dark floral pattern, replace them with a set in a lighter print. Take the concept a step further by applying it to table skirts and throw pillows, too.

▲ A RED AND GREEN COLOR SCHEME won't look like Christmas if you choose the right tints and shades. In this eating area, Kelly green walls provide a spirited backdrop for the country-style setting, complete with a red and white checked tablecloth. White built-ins and even the chairs add visual balance.

FLOORS AND CEILINGS

▶ IN SHADES OF HUNTER GREEN, rust, and buttery cream, this color-blocked sectional and matching chair couldn't have a better companion than the contemporary rug that anchors the area. It repeats not only specific colors but also the shapes of the cushions.

▼ THE PRIMARY COLORS throughout this playroom are firmly grounded with an area rug that picks up the reds, yellows, and blues. But the floor covering also serves another purpose—it provides a softer play space than does the ceramic tile beneath it.

Choosing the Right Paint

WHEN IT COMES TO CHOOSING the right kind of paint, the options can be confusing. Oil-base paint is one possibility, but if you don't have professional experience, it's best to stick with latex (water-base) paint because it's easier to clean up afterwards. There are several choices, however, within the category of latex paint—flat, eggshell, satin, semi-gloss, and high gloss. The finishes range from matte to shiny and the washability from not at all to scrubbable. Most often, eggshell is the best choice for walls and semigloss for moldings and trim. They'll give you the right amount of sheen and can still be wiped free of marks and fingerprints.

▲ CLOUDS PAINTED ON THE CEILING are nothing new, but the ones in this dining room take the art to a higher level. A combination of white, ochre, and sky blue hues has been applied to give this artistic sky a bit of a three-dimensional look.

◄ IN ADDITION TO THE CLOUDS on this dining room ceiling, delicate floral bouquets have been hand-painted between each pair of Palladian windows. The walls themselves have a decorative faux finish; also in ochre, they provide a visual bridge to the ceiling above.

Furniture

The furniture that you choose for your home can serve as a starting point for your decorating scheme, providing a palette of favorite colors or the beginnings of a specific style. Or it can be inspired by a distinctive element that you already have—an Oriental rug found at an antiques store, a drop-lid desk with a decorative paint finish, even a contemporary work of art.

Although aesthetics play an important part in furniture selection, there's more to consider than just good looks. A piece needs to please the eye, but also provide comfort and complement your personal sense of style. Above all, it should suit your lifestyle. If you're laid-back, consider a sofa conducive to sprawling out on; if you're more formal, opt for wingback chairs with sit-up-straight support.

Good construction is another key consideration. Doors and drawers should glide easily and have interlocking joinery as opposed to a frame built from wood pieces simply butted together. Upholstery can be a bit more difficult to evaluate initially, but don't be timid; pick up that sofa or chair and turn it over to look for a sturdy frame and springs.

◄ THE DEEP CINNAMON SHADE OF THIS SOFA, picked up from the area rug, anchors the conversation area. Its solid color—vibrant against a stark white wall—emphasizes its graceful shape, which is a welcome contrast to the straight-lined window, shade, and artwork directly behind it.

Sofas

A SOFA IS ONE OF THE LARGEST PIECES OF FURNITURE in a room—and one of the largest investments you'll make. As a result, you'll want one with classic lines and a color that you'll be comfortable living with for years to come. That doesn't mean that you can't change the look, however. A quick switch of decorative pillows can transform it in a matter of minutes. On a solid gold sofa, for instance, pillows in subtle shades of cream will lend an air of quiet elegance. Replace them with bright red pillows and you instantly inject excitement into the room.

Before you bring a sofa home, though, make sure that it fits into the room and the front door. (They're usually between 7 ft. and 8 ft. long.) If you have a smaller space, you may want to opt for a loveseat—or two. Set the pair so that they face each other and add a coffee table in between to create a cozy grouping.

▲ SMALL ROOMS call for seating that's suitable in scale. An apartment-size sofa like the one in this living room is larger than a love seat but smaller than a conventional sofa. In a cream color, it gets plenty of attention against the dramatically dark walls.

◀ A CONTEMPORARY CAMELBACK SOFA with a reverse center "hump" adds soft curves to this living room. The piece provides a good balancing act with the end table, leather chair, and area rug, all of which are more square or rectangular.

▲ A CORAL SOFA is the center of attention in this room. The seating piece, just a shade lighter than the curtains behind it, features an assortment of patterned pillows, keeping things visually interesting in a space where almost everything else is in a solid color.

TRICKS OF THE TRADE

Pillow Talk

A NEW SOFA TYPICALLY COMES WITH A PAIR OF MATCHING THROW PILLOWS. While they provide extra comfort they can also get lost, visually, against the sofa's identical pattern and color. To make things more interesting, look around the room. If there's a pair of upholstered chairs with matching pillows of their own, put those on the sofa and vice versa; in a well-coordinated room, the fabrics should blend beautifully. If there are no other pillows in the room with which you can make a switch, simply add two more pillows to the original pair; just make sure that they're in a contrasting pattern and, for variety, slightly larger, too.

SOFA STYLES

When shopping for a sofa, you'll find that there's a wealth from which to choose. For the most part, however, they can be categorized into three basic styles.

CAMELBACK

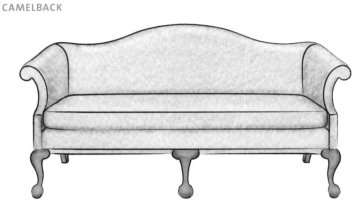

A camelback sofa, often used in formal settings, has a serpentine line that rises from the arms to a high point in the middle of the back.

LAWSON

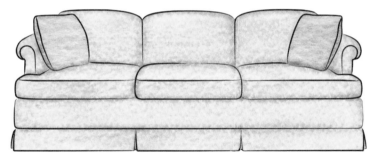

A Lawson sofa, which can be casual or formal, has rolled arms that reach halfway between the seat and the top of its back, which is either straight across or slightly arched. Typically, it is skirted, too.

TUXEDO

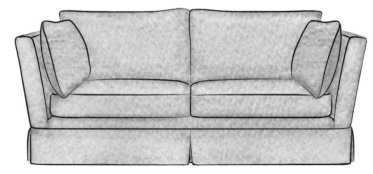

A tuxedo sofa is clean lined and contemporary. It features slightly flared arms that are the same height as the back.

▲ THE WOOD FRAME of this sofa is perfectly suited to the rest of the room's primitive furnishings. Its low profile doesn't block the view outside the windows, either, where changing seasons provide the artwork.

Shopping for Sofa Beds

SOFA BEDS ARE NO LONGER FITTED WITH PAPER-THIN MATTRESSES and supported with crossbars that keep you awake at night. Today's versions have smooth operating mechanisms, comfortable mattresses, and stylish designs. A good sofa bed should pass the same quality tests as any piece of upholstery. As for the mattress, look for one that's 4-½ in. to 5 in. thick; the thickness should come from the springs inside, though, and not from extra padding on top that will compress over time. Full- and queen-size sofa beds are readily available but you'll also find twin-size mattresses set into oversize chairs.

▲ YELLOWS AND GOLDS PREDOMINATE HERE, but it's the brilliant red hue of a few pieces that sets the mood. Had the sofa matched its surroundings, the room would have had a more formal feeling. The bright red—cued from decorative pillows and a footstool—establishes an electrifying atmosphere.

LOVESEATS

▲ LOVESEATS ARE A GOOD OPTION in the bedroom, where seating space is often at a premium. Set at a right angle next to a fireplace, this loveseat takes advantage of the fire's warmth without putting its back to the bed on its other side.

◄ THIS SPOTTED CAMELBACK LOVESEAT stands out prominently against a subtle beige and white striped wallpaper and equally understated sisal floor covering. Its convertible arms can be lowered to seat level, turning the piece into a comfortable sleeping spot for overnight guests.

▼ IN A LIGHT-FILLED ROOM, black grounds a scheme like no other color. In this living room, a pair of black leather loveseats faces off in front of a wood-burning stove, each providing a clear view of the fire as well as the view beyond.

ABOUT ARMS

The shape of a sofa arm contributes more to its style than you might think. The rolled arm, for example, is more comfortable and casual while others, like the English arm have a more formal flair.

PLEATED

A pleated arm features fabric that pleats and comes to a single point where the front of the arm meets the side of the sofa.

ENGLISH

An English arm, also known as a Charles of London arm—with a serpentine styling—is pleated along the outside edge, where the arm meets the side of the sofa.

ROLLED

A rolled arm is a continuation of the sofa's side, scrolling around to form a near-cylindrical form. Its thick padding makes it one of the most comfortable arm styles.

▶ SECTIONAL SOFAS are a particularly good choice for growing families. This one, upholstered in a durable fabric, fits neatly into a corner now but can be reconfigured when it's time to move it to a different home or simply a different room.

▲ A STEPPED-DOWN CONVERSATION PIT creates a cozy feeling. Here, a sectional is positioned at opposing corners. The larger piece is made up of two sofa-length pieces, while the smaller one is composed of a matching chaise. There's just enough room between the two for steps leading down to the area.

The Inside Story on Upholstery

YOU DON'T HAVE TO BE SUPERMAN™ to see the construction beneath a piece of upholstery. Start by examining the frame. Kiln-dried hardwoods such as maple or hickory are more durable than soft woods like pine. Next, make sure that the legs are sturdy; they should be a continuation of the frame, not separate pieces that have been nailed or screwed on. Joints should be a combination of wooden dowels and metal screws and/or buttressed with corner blocks. And springs, preferably eight-way hand-tied, should be made of tempered steel. (Eight-way hand-tied springs are secured to the eight surrounding springs with heavy, knotted twine.) Finally, make sure that the upholstery and padding thoroughly covers the inner springs so that you can't see—or feel—them.

▲ IN OPEN FLOOR PLANS, sectional sofas in L-shaped configurations create a sense of boundaries. This sectional is the cornerstone of the main living area. Teamed with a coffee table, an area rug, and two leather chairs, it completes an intimate grouping—and keeps the view out the windows in sight.

Chairs

CHAIRS HAVE JUST AS MANY SHAPES AND STYLES AS THEY DO USES. There's "your" chair at the breakfast table, where you read the newspaper each morning. There are club chairs where you settle for cozy conversation, wingback chairs where you sit and admire a fire, and chaises where you stretch out for an afternoon nap. There are also those referred to as a chair and a half, large enough to accommodate a parent and child (or, some say, a man and a dog). That's not to mention all of the other options, from diminutive accent chairs that are at home in the living room to benches that work just as well in the entry as they do at the foot of the bed. There's even a wide variety of recliners; some have their mechanisms so well hidden they're hard to identify as recliners at all. No matter how big or small, however, comfort must be part of the equation. Before buying any chair, take it for the ultimate test drive—sit on it.

▲ DEPENDING ON THEIR color and pattern, fabrics can communicate a masculine or feminine feeling. The overstuffed nature of this chair immediately gives it a comfortable feeling. At the same time, though, it's feminine—thanks to the floral fabric, pleated skirt, and pink contrasting welting.

◄ BIG AND BOXY, this chair and a half in a fiery orange fabric warms up a cool gray concrete wall. The accompanying ottoman even adds an element of warmth. Although green is a cool color, this shade has enough yellow in it, to complement the chair rather than contrast with it.

▼ THIS LEATHER-COVERED CLUB CHAIR, with its gracefully scrolled arms and back as well as stylish splayed legs, is the perfect reading retreat. Like here, it's important that every seat in a room have adequate lighting and a place to set a beverage or snack.

SKIRT STYLES

Upholstery offers an entire wardrobe of skirts from which to choose. As in fashion, however, it's important to match the "body type" with the right skirt. Pleated styles are most appropriate for tailored seating pieces. Chairs with more curves, covered in lighter-weight cottons, lend themselves more to softly gathered styles.

TUXEDO

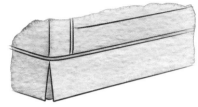

Tuxedo skirts feature a single pleat at each corner.

GATHERED

Gathered skirts consist of one continuous ruffle around the bottom edge.

DRESSMAKER

Dressmaker skirts also consist of one continuous ruffle but are applied on the outside and typically feature some kind of decorative welting to cover the line of stitching.

Give 'em the Slip

SLIPCOVERS HAVE A CHAMELEON-LIKE QUALITY, **allowing you to change the personality of a sofa or chair in no time at all. If you're throwing a dinner party**, for instance, dress every-day dining chairs with elegant slipcovers to create a more formal mood. Or take a cue from Mother Nature and celebrate the changing seasons. Keep different sets of slipcovers on hand for upholstered sofas and chairs—in lightweight linen for spring, a canvas cloth for summer, heavy cotton for fall, and warm corduroy for winter.

Custom slipcovers can fit your sofa or chair like a second skin or drape over the piece loosely. But custom covers aren't the only choice you have. Some manufacturers offer the option of buying them when you purchase your piece of furniture. Plus, there are plenty of ready-made slipcovers that can be "custom fitted" by adjusting an elastic edge or bow tie. Perhaps the greatest benefit of slipcovers, however, is that they're typically made of a durable material that can withstand repeated washings.

▲ A PAIR OF GREEN-AND-RED PLAID armchairs, set in front of a wood-paneled wall, creates a quintessential library look. Strategically positioned on an angle, the chairs allow occupants to get a glimpse of the grand fireplace but still be a part of the main conversation group.

◄ HIS-AND-HERS CHAIRS IN A SUBTLE STRIPE unite all of the colors in this living room. Their deeply tufted backs make it apparent that comfort is a high priority, as does the ottoman that can be used by one occupant or the other—or even shared.

▲ USE SLIPCOVERS ACCORDING TO THE SEASON. Here, white canvas slipcovers establish a refreshing summer-time feeling. And cleaning consists of nothing more than throwing them in the wash. When cooler weather rolls around, the slipcovers are simply pulled off to reveal upholstery in warmer tones.

CHAISES

▶ IN A ROOM WITH MINIMAL FURNITURE, each piece takes on more importance. That's the case here, where a contemporary chaise is set dramatically close to the stone fireplace. It's not set so close that the fireplace can't be used, though, allowing the occupant to warm up while enjoying the view.

▲ THIS GLAMOROUS CHAISE is positioned to take advantage of the spectacular view. Its unique mechanism allows you to sit up or recline back, depending on what position you find most comfortable.

TRICKS OF THE TRADE

Choosing Cushion Fill

SELECTING AN UPHOLSTERED PIECE OF FURNITURE is similar to buying a car: The color is important, but it's what you find under the hood that counts. That's where cushion fill comes in—what makes the seat so comfortable. Good-quality foam provides firm support and always looks tidy, but won't last as long as steel springs combined with synthetic fiberfill, feathers, or down, each one with an increasingly higher level of sink-into comfort. Down cushions are the most plush, but require regular fluffing to keep them looking neat. Instead, you may want to opt for combination spring/down cushions that offer solid support and luxurious softness.

▲ A BENTWOOD CHAISE in this living room offers more than a comfortable place to recline. From a visual point of view, it provides an interesting textural contrast to the upholstered sofa, thick-pile rug, and a concrete block-fireplace—and is a piece of sculpture in its own right.

ACCENT CHAIRS

▼ CONTEMPORARY SIDE CHAIRS in this entry establish a light-hearted attitude. The whimsical fabric on the seats and backs sets the mood and draws attention thanks to the pale blond chair frames and striped walls. Here, the chairs are intended as resting spots, not places to spend long amounts of time.

▲ THIS SITTING SPOT is a study in eye-appealing contrasts. The pale wood frame of this fireside chair diametrically opposes the jet black webbed seat while, in turn, the curvaceous profile of the chair does the same to the more hard-lined fireplace.

A Personal Touch

YOU DON'T HAVE TO BE an interior designer to utilize one of the professionals' best tricks. That is, when placing an order for an upholstered chair—whether it's fully upholstered or simply has a fabric seat—ask if "COM" is an option. This designation refers to the "customer's own material," which can be selected from a group of fabrics offered by the chair manufacturer or provided by the customer, having been purchased from a separate source. For that matter, "COM" is an option for many upholstered pieces, from the smallest footstool to sectional sofas.

▶ PLUMP SEAT CUSHIONS soften these wicker armchairs. Plus, the contrasting colors of the two elements make the textures of each more distinct. The softening effect is taken yet a step further with the table that serves them both; the round shape is the perfect counterpoint to the chairs' angular silhouettes.

DINING CHAIRS

▲ COUNTER-HEIGHT CHAIRS in the same bright white as this kitchen's cabinetry would have been bland.
These, however—in a contrasting dark wood finish—add a touch of warmth that draws you immediately to
this sun-filled space.

◄ MIXING STYLES AND COLORS is a sure way to create a one-of-a-kind look. These cream-colored Windsor chairs are silhouetted beautifully against a cherry Shaker-style table. Although the styles aren't identical they work together because they're from the same Early American era.

▼ IN A KITCHEN full of straight edges and hard angles, these contemporary counter stools are a welcome reprieve. The shapely backs echo the light woods found throughout the room but the circular seats, in a darker hue, keep them firmly grounded, too.

▼ DINING CHAIRS NEED NOT BE FULLY UPHOLSTERED to be completely relaxing. The frames of these match the wood of the table while upholstered seats and backs provide plenty of comfort. The wood tones, in fact, find their way up to the ceiling, where paneling emphasizes the barrel shape.

▲ A VARIETY OF PATTERNS can be right at home together, as long as they have some colors in common. Dining chairs in striped upholstery set a traditional mood in this room, their earthy colors emphasized further by an Oriental rug and fireplace tiles on the nearby hearth.

Mixing Dining Chairs

PERFECTLY MATCHED SUITES OF FURNITURE aren't the only option for today's dining rooms. Once you've selected a table, mix and match chairs to create a one-of-a-kind ambiance. Start with variations on a specific style. If, for instance, you have country-style tendencies, surround your table with an assortment of Windsor chairs, ranging from the rounded bow-back Windsor to its splayed fan-back counterpart. To mix things up in a more traditional setting, use matching chairs along the sides of the table but distinctly different host and hostess chairs at each end. The side chairs, for example, might have wooden frames with upholstered seats and backs while the host and hostess chairs might be fully upholstered wingbacks, covered in a fabric that complements the smaller side chairs. It's in contemporary spaces, however, that you can have the most fun. Settle on a specific chair style, perhaps one with a metal frame, and then upholster the seats and backs of each chair in a different hue.

▲ THESE DIVERSE DINING CHAIRS work together because they all incorporate a coral color. A paisley on the host and hostess chairs features the same kinds of curves as the chair frames. Armless chairs, in solids and prints, are a good choice along the sides so multiple arms don't get entangled.

OTTOMANS

▲ IN ADDITION TO SERVING AS A COMFORTABLE PLACE to prop your feet, an ottoman can stand in for a conventional coffee table. Here, a round, fully upholstered piece provides a convenient place to set a tray of beverages or stack a few books.

Pet-Friendly Fabrics

WITH PETS MORE POPULAR THAN EVER before, it's comforting to know that there are fabrics that are just as well suited to family as they are to our furry friends. A new generation of "performance" fabrics is durable, stain resistant, and easy to clean. What's more, they don't give up a thing in terms of style. Ultrasuede™ falls into this category as do microfibers; with tightly woven fibers that repel moisture easily, they're good choices for upholstery and even slipcovers. Not only can they be easily spot-cleaned but some can even be thrown in the wash. These fabrics may cost a bit more initially than standard upholstery fabrics but they will last longer, too, making them cheaper in the long run.

▲ NEARLY SPANNING THE LENGTH of the sofa that it accompanies, this rectangular ottoman doubles the number of people that can be seated in this space. But it's more than a purely functional piece; its striped fabric was the impetus for the room's color scheme.

◄ A FOREST GREEN OTTOMAN draws the eye immediately into this seating area, where other large furnishings are in off-white neutral hues. Set on casters, the ottoman can move closer to the seating pieces for TV dinners or farther away to serve as supplementary seating.

BENCHES

◄ USED IN LIEU OF A MORE CONVEN-TIONAL SOFA OR LOVESEAT, a pair of red, square benches completes this seating group, taking up less visual room in a place where space is at a premium. Because they're lightweight, they're easy to move to accommodate parties or general traffic flow.

▼ THIS CUSHIONED BENCH, tucked into a stair landing, would be inviting on its own but is even more so thanks to the piles of pillows. With protective railings on either side, it's a good place for kids to read or play. Plus, it doubles as storage space.

◄ A WOODEN BENCH, painted a soft shade of green, is practical in more ways than one. It not only offers a sitting spot but also minimizes the radiator behind it. The exact same width as the radiator and the window, the bench is seemingly custom-built for the spot.

▼ THIS WOODEN BENCH, sculptural in its simplicity, runs the length of the display shelf above it, tying together the furniture and the artwork above it. The wooden seat also serves as a display space of its own, providing a warm brown backdrop for decorative items.

Tables

THINK OF TABLES and your mind immediately goes to the kitchen or dining room. But there is a wealth of other versatile options. Tables come in all types of configurations and sizes, styles, colors, and materials. In fact, tables can be changed out from one room to the next, providing a new decorating scheme without spending any money. The lamp table beside a chair today might be at home next to your bed tomorrow. Likewise, the slim console table that provides a drop-off spot for keys in the foyer can also back up to a sofa, showcasing family photographs.

In a room with several table types, traditionalists may prefer that they all be of the same wood—oak or cherry, for instance. But an eclectic approach can often better reflect a homeowner's personality. If they have classic lines and similar styles you can mix and match table types to your heart's content, even including designs that are painted or made of metal.

▲ WHETHER IT'S IN COLOR, TEXTURE, OR FORM, contrast makes a room more visually interesting. This trio of accent tables covers all the angles. Not only do their various geometric forms provide a change of pace; the black leather tops and dark rattan bases stand out against the much-lighter wicker chairs.

◄ THERE'S SOMETHING APPEALING about a kitchen that's spic and span, even more so when it is all white. The absence of color here allows accessories to create the excitement, including a pitcher of flowers and a wrought iron chandelier, both of which lead the eye—and guests—to the table.

▲ THIS MODERN-DAY VERSION of a Victorian tea table (just the right height for sipping tea) offers practicality; its drop leaves can be extended for serving refreshments of any kind. Although it has a different finish, this table works well with the nearby lamp table because they both have eighteenth-century roots.

FORMAL DINING

▶ SOME OF THE MOST EXCITING ROOM SCHEMES are the result of opposites attracting. In this eclectic dining room, a contemporary table and chairs provide a sleek counterpoint for traditional architecture. Their wood frames capture attention while the white room fades away quietly, allowing the two styles to complement, not clash.

▶ THE ARCHITECTURAL STYLE of a home need not always dictate the style of the furnishings within. This contemporary home, complete with a dynamic version of beamed ceiling, is trimmed out in light woods, allowing the darker, Oriental-style dining table and chairs to take the spotlight.

▲ THERE CAN BE TOO MUCH of a good thing, pattern being a prime example. Amid a stone wall, an Oriental rug, and a beautiful view, this simple wood table and the Windsor chairs that surround it are simple—a breath of fresh air, in a decorative sense.

▲ IN ANOTHER SETTING, this dining table and chairs would have taken on a more formal feeling. But here, the eating area is open to the nearby kitchen giving the ensemble a more casual flair.

▼ A ROUND DINING TABLE makes it easier to converse with dinner companions. And the one in this room has another advantage: Its pedestal base ensures extra room for the legs of the chairs—and the diners.

Size Matters

SHOPPING FOR A DINING ROOM TABLE involves more than deciding on a shape and a style. Size is also an important consideration, not only in terms of what will fit into your room but also what will fit your family's lifestyle, whether it's laid-back or more formal. In any case, your table should allow between 24 in. and 30 in. per person from side to side and approximately 30 in. deep. If any of the dining chairs fall in front of a table leg, however, allow enough extra room so that the person in front of it can comfortably move to one side or the other.

◀ FORMAL DINING ROOMS don't have to be fussy. This one is decked out in an unpretentious white table and chairs, accompanied by a matching cupboard. The addition of a crystal chandelier and lamp, though, adds just the right touch of sparkle to the room.

▼ IN THIS FORMAL DINING ROOM, neutral hues establish an air of elegance, while a variety of textures—from the smooth glass-top table to the coarsely woven fabric on the dining room chairs—add interest, keeping the tone-on-tone scheme from falling flat.

CASUAL DINING

▲ BECAUSE THE ARCHITECTURE IN THIS DINING ROOM is so strong, furnishings were kept intentionally simple. The table and chairs are a study in contrasts, teaming up black-painted finishes with pale woods. Set against light yellow walls, they gain additional stature.

Stretching Exercises

BEFORE PURCHASING A DINING TABLE, consider whether it will occasionally need to expand to accommodate more family and friends. Not only do many rectangular tables come with leaves but so do their round counterparts; some have conventional leaves that can turn a round table into an oval-shaped one and there are even a few that, with pie-shaped inserts, can give a round table a larger circumference.

In the past, extra table leaves were typically stashed in a closet when not in use. Today, more often than not, they're conveniently stored under—or within—the tabletop itself.

▲ THIS MODERN MID-TWENTIETH-CENTURY DINING SET still has fresh appeal. The shapely forms of the all-white table and bent plywood chairs are even more evident with ever-so-slight contrasting colors in the blonde floor and walls in a pale gray-green shade.

▶ THE TRADITIONAL ARCHITECTURE AND TABLE in this casual dining room are offset with the style, material, and even color of the wicker chairs. The wooden top of the farmhouse table ties together the various hues, all from the same color family.

ABOUT LEGS AND FEET

Sofas and chairs with exposed legs take on a lighter, airier appearance. You'll find dozens of different styles, but here are the most common types:

BALL-AND-CLAW FOOT

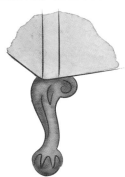

A ball-and-claw foot resembles the claw of a bird or animal grasping a ball.

BUN FOOT

The bun foot is almost round but flattened just a bit on the top and bottom. It can be made of wood or covered in fabric to match the seating piece.

CABRIOLE LEG

A cabriole leg can be identified by its "S" shape, curving outward at the knee, back in as it moves down the leg, and out again just above the foot.

MARLBOROUGH LEG

The Marlborough leg is straight and square. Embellishment is kept to a minimum, too, sometimes with either fluting (vertically carved grooves) or a horizontal "stop" near the bottom of the leg.

▲ SOMETIMES THE MOST CREATIVE DESIGN SOLUTIONS come from the challenges at hand. In this kitchen, a small corner wasn't large enough for a conventional breakfast table and chairs. Built-ins fit in neatly, though. The mix of materials—wood, aluminum, glass, even concrete—provide a modern twist on the 1950s banquette.

Surface Matters

FROM A PRACTICAL POINT OF VIEW, **eat-in kitchens require tables with easy-to-clean surfaces. Glass tops are** one option, either see-through or frosted (if you prefer not to look down and see your feet). Laminates are another alternative; if they're suitable for use as countertops they can stand up to the daily use of tabletops, too. Built-in tables, particularly, lend themselves to laminates. Plus, you can select a pattern that matches or complements other surfaces in the room.

That's not to say that a conventional wooden table can't be appropriate, too. Just be sure that it has a protective surface such as polyurethane or wax. Either will give you a little time to clean up spills before they cause permanent damage.

▲ FLANKING THIS TABLE are built-in banquettes with a casual nature, including bright green cushions, red and white striped pillows, even drawers tucked in the bottom of each. The setting is topped off with an equally creative display of mittens and gloves in brilliant hues.

▲ THANKS TO COMMON RED, PURPLE, AND NEUTRAL HUES, contemporary furnishings are right at home with a pair of armchairs that have traditional frames. But the tables are the stars here; a black and white cube, acrylic coffee table, and a red lacquer and metal side table are all sculptural in their own right.

▲ TWIN BEDS IN A ROOM can take up a fair amount of space, leaving little for other essential pieces. One of the keys is to think small; another is to look for shared opportunities. This petite pedestal table with a reading lamp serves both sleeping spots.

A Means to an End Table

As the name implies, an end table takes its place at the end, or one side, of a sofa, chair, or bed. First and foremost, it should complement the piece that it accompanies, but that doesn't mean it has to match. Contemporary tables can work with traditional chairs while painted versions can complement a bed with rich wood finishes. If you have a small room, the limited floor space needs to be considered, too. Pedestal tables have a smaller "footprint" than solid cubes or nesting tables that, until called into use, stack one atop the other.

▲ A SQUARE-TOP PEDESTAL TABLE fits neatly into the corner of this room, coupled with a wicker chair that provides contrast in color and texture. The dark hue creates a focal point, inviting you to sit down and enjoy the impressive ocean view.

Skirting the Issue

AROUND TABLE CAN PROVIDE A WELCOME CHANGE OF PACE in a room full of rectangular sofas, square-shaped chairs, and boxy window treatments. To further soften the effect, you can dress it up in any number of ways.

- Use an opaque floor-length tablecloth. Because the table is completely covered, it doesn't have to be the best one that you have.

- Place a topper over a floor-length skirt, changing it from season to season for a variety of looks. The topper, a square piece of fabric at least 6 in. wider than the diameter of the table, can be simply hemmed or given a contrasting trim.

- Dress a handsome round table with a skirt made of see-through organza to keep things light and airy during the warm summer months. The table's silhouette will show up better if it's made of a dark wood.

▲ WHAT COULD HAVE BEEN A PLAIN SKIRT on this table becomes striking with the addition of a simple trim. The bullion fringe at the bottom edge adds just the right amount of textural interest that is important in a neutral scheme.

◀ LAYERED OVER A SKIRT, a square piece of fabric, known as a topper, can add an extra dimension of color and pattern to a table. Here, a plaid topper with red trim ties together the sage green hue of the walls and the red of the sofa, upholstered chair, and window treatments.

▲ THIS PEDESTAL TABLE has a warm wood finish that balances the cooler neutrals of the sofa and armchair that it serves. End tables shouldn't be more than 2 in. higher or lower than the arm of the nearby seat, making it easy to reach a book or beverage.

CONSOLE TABLES

▼ GRACEFULLY CURVED LEGS on the base of this console table draw the eye to its sculptural form. The curvilinear base also provides a sharp contrast to the more linear top, which has a lattice rail to keep items within the tabletop's bounds.

◄ THE SLIM CONSOLE TABLE in this hallway is as much a work of art as the sculpture on top of it or the artwork above. The simple but striking lines of this rich wood piece, matching the hardwood floor, are even more evident against the bright white wall.

▼ SET CROSSWAYS in a large room, a sofa can divide it into two smaller spaces. This console table placed in back of it further defines the boundaries while serving both areas. It provides an appealing tablescape on one side and holds lamps that provide reading light for the other.

COFFEE TABLES

▲ NOT ONLY IS THE SYMMETRY SOOTHING in this living room but the cool colors are, too. Because the sofas are set far enough apart to flank the expansive fireplace, two slim coffee tables—or one larger square—are needed so that both are accommodated.

▶ THE FINISH of this black lacquered table with gold decorative accents is eye catching on its own, but the exaggerated cabriole legs make it even more so. Other furnishings in the room are quietly neutral in hue, allowing the piece to prominently take center stage.

◄ THE BEAUTY OF GLASS-TOP TABLES, like this square version, is that they take up very little visual space, allowing the eye to see right through them. In this case, that allows you to fully appreciate the sculptured table legs and carpet pattern below.

▼ THIS ROOM USES TWO SMALLER SQUARE TABLES. That way, they can be moved wherever they're needed most. The reddish hue of the tables grounds the conversation area; tables in a lighter tone would have caused the pastel grouping to become visually lost within the room.

Table Scale

WHEN SELECTING A COFFEE TABLE, it's important to consider size as much as style. One that's too small will look out of proportion and won't serve the seating pieces well, either; everyone sitting around the table should be able to easily reach a beverage or snack. To keep things in scale, look for a coffee table that's approximately two-thirds as long as the sofa itself. That will allow an easy reach for everyone in the conversation group and provide adequate space to walk around the table at each end. Keep in mind, too, that a coffee table of the appropriate size will leave room for treasured collectibles and accessories.

▲ A TRADITIONAL COFFEE TABLE would have been expected in this conversation grouping but this more artistic one, with a rough-hewn look, adds a welcome element of surprise. Plus, it provides a tie, stylistically, to the stone fireplace.

▼ THESE TWO TABLES in staggered heights offer multiple possibilities. A rectangular version and its shorter square counterpart team up to form a two-level configuration here but—thanks to their light weight—can be pulled apart and moved wherever they're most needed in the room.

▲ IN FAMILY ROOMS, coffee tables are best if they serve more than one purpose. This hardworking version has the requisite tabletop surface with a shallow display space for collectibles beneath it. Additionally, drawers around the base provide room for assorted items that need to be close at hand.

ACCENT TABLES

▲ THE ULTIMATE SPACE SAVERS, nesting tables like these can tuck neatly beneath one another. But pulled apart even slightly, in this kind of stair-step fashion, they have a sculptural quality all their own.

Painted Furniture

OR A ONE-OF-A-KIND PIECE OF FURNITURE, paint it with a finish of your own creation. Unfinished furnishings make good candidates, as do those that have seen better days or flea market finds. Be sure, though, to do the prep work first. Sand the wood until it's smooth (or as smooth as you want it to be) and then prime the surface. Once the primer is dry, you're ready to paint.

Furniture painted in solid colors, stripes, and even checks can easily be coordinated with a room. But the possibilities are endless. In a room full of antiques, painted furnishings with crackle finishes fit right in because the process instantly "ages" a piece. Distressing is another way to get an antique look, especially if you batter the furniture before painting it by making indentations with things like nails and small pieces of chain. Whatever look you like, you can probably achieve it with paint.

▲ ACCENT TABLES can be handsome and practical. This example, conveniently close to the armchair, provides for practicality, but its brass rail brings it into the decorative realm. Like the nearby artwork and chair, the table is traditional in style. The chair's contemporary upholstery, though, gives the traditional setting a twist.

▲ THIS TABLE GETS A NEW LEASE ON LIFE with paint applied in a creative way. The tabletop and the legs were painted and then had some of the finish rubbed away for an aged appearance. The table's apron echoes the wall's warm hue.

▲ SIMPLE CUBES fulfill the requirement of any accent table—surface space. This pair is upholstered to match the cushions in the window seat. Cut-to-fit glass tops protect the fabric while making the tabletop easy to clean, too.

Beds

Y OU'VE HEARD IT BEFORE: We spend no less than one-third of our lives in bed. It's no wonder, then, that choosing one is such an important decision. But it is a step-by-step process. The first decision to be made is size, anywhere from a twin to a king and, after that, the softness or firmness of the mattress. When it comes to a particular type, though, you can make a personal statement. From draped canopies to gleaming metals, you'll find beds in every imaginable style. Though steeped in tradition, four-posters can be contemporary, too. And sleigh beds have moved beyond beautifully carved wood to encompass metal, wicker, and even upholstery. Be sure that the bed you choose fits into your room, from the standpoint not of only mattress size but height as well. Once you get it through the door, you don't want to find that it's too tall or that it visually overwhelms the space.

▲ A CANOPY SUSPENDED FROM THE WALL can dress up any bed. The gathered fabric that forms the back of this canopy matches that of the tied-back curtains flanking it. The elaborate valance and finials, though, are the central focus, the gold trim on each echoed on the round bolster bed pillows.

◄ ELEVATING THE HEIGHT OF A BED can make it seem all the more impressive. This canopy goes a step further, too, with gauzy bed curtains tied with oversize tassels. Underscoring it—as well as the bedside tables—is a sisal rug that defines the sleeping spot.

▲ ALL-WHITE LINENS on an intricately carved four-poster like this allow the bed itself to take the spotlight; the spiral-shaped posts and scalloped headboard are ornate without being overdone. The dark wood makes the bed stand out, too, set against an entirely neutral backdrop.

◄ IN A ROOM WITH GREAT ARCHITECTURE, simplified furnishings are often best, allowing the architecture to shine. The dropped molding in this bedroom, even more evident against mocha walls, creates a more intimate feeling. The simple four-poster has an espresso wood finish that's silhouetted beautifully against the lighter hue.

▲ THE SHORTENED FOUR-POSTER in this bedroom is a good choice as it doesn't interfere with the breathtaking ocean view. The bed's bamboo-like trim, plus simple bed linens, add to the breezy appeal.

▶ INTRICATELY CARVED FURNISHINGS are showcased best against solid-color backgrounds. That's apparent in this bedroom, where a four-poster seems almost sculptural against pale green walls. The tall posts, with their pointed finials, draw attention to one of the room's best architectural features— a domed ceiling.

◄ THE UNDERSTATED, UPHOLSTERED HEAD-BOARD of this bed visually balances the elaborately carved posts. Meanwhile, bed linens in soft, cool hues establish a sense of calm while surrounding furnishings—eclectic bed-side tables, mirrors, and an ottoman that all have a traditional theme—offer richness with intricate patterns and designs.

Mattress Sizes

THERE ARE ONLY TWO FACTORS in selecting a mattress size. First, determine what you have room for, allowing approximately 2 ft. of space on the sides and at the foot so you can easily make the bed each day. After that, concentrate on comfort. Most people are more comfortable in queen- or even king-size beds. There are accommodations for those who are tall, as well. In a California king, you'll give up a few inches in width but gain a valuable 4 in. in length. Here are the most common mattress measurements:

- Twin: 38 in. by 75 in.
- Extra-long twin: 38 in. by 80 in.
- Double, Standard, Full: 54 in. by 75 in.
- Queen: 60 in. by 80 in.
- King: 76 in. by 80 in.
- California king: 72 in. by 84 in.

SLEIGH BEDS

▼ PLACING A BED ON AN ANGLE immediately gives it a greater presence. This metal sleigh bed gets even more attention thanks to the contrasting tones of the dark frame and lighter bed linens. The metal is also a welcome mix to the other textures in this neutral room.

▲ NAMED AFTER the horse-drawn sleighs that they resemble, sleigh beds have an innate feeling of comfort. This traditional carved-wood version has side rails that disguise the bed's box springs, thus eliminating the need to dress them like the rest of the bed.

Test-Drive a Mattress

THERE'S ONLY ONE WAY TO FIND THE MATTRESS THAT'S RIGHT FOR YOU: **Lie on it.** Before you make a purchase, get dressed in comfortable clothing and take several models for a "test drive." If you share a bed with someone, it's important that he or she try out the mattress, too. Lie on it in your typical sleeping position, then move around a little. If you read in bed, check it out in a sitting position, too. Just keep in mind that a firm mattress is not always the best mattress. Instead, it's a matter of personal preference and what feels right to you.

▼ A SMALL PLAID PRINT is a pleasing contrast to the curves of this upholstered sleigh bed. Shades of green are repeated on the bedside table and the area rug. It's a rosy pink rocker and quilt, however, which keep the cool scheme from turning cold.

METAL BEDS

▶ NEUTRAL COLORS are naturally soothing, making them appropriate for any bedroom. This bedroom features a metal bed painted a white hue, which reappears on the walls, the bed linens, and other furnishings. The neutral hues lighten and brighten the small space, making it seem bigger than its actual dimensions.

▼ DISPELLING THE NOTION that metal beds are all hard-edged, this fanciful version takes scrollwork to a new level. Solid-color bed linens are mandatory here, as a print would detract from the bed. A small Oriental rug adds pattern by incorporating scrollwork of its own.

The Well-Stocked Linen Closet

TO KEEP ALL OF THE BED COVERINGS you need readily at your fingertips, it's important to keep a well-stocked linen closet. For starters, be sure that you have at least two sets of sheets for every bed in the house. Two pillows per person is a good idea, too. Other essentials for each bed include a mattress cover, pillowcase protectors, which can be washed more easily than pillows, as well as one summer and one winter blanket. Beyond that, it's a matter of the decorative dressings that you prefer, from comforters and coverlets to quilts and spreads.

▲ SIMPLE SCARVES, draped asymmetrically over this metal frame bed, create a casual ambiance. Their white hue blends quietly into the background; had they been in a more vibrant color, the bed would have been more imposing.

DAYBEDS

▼ BUILT-IN DAYBEDS not only lend a more tailored look; but also provide the opportunity for under-the-bed storage, whether it's for extra bed linens or out-of-season clothing. These daybeds are backed with standard bed pillows so there's no need to keep them stashed in a nearby closet.

▲ DOUBLING AS A SOFA AND A SLEEPING SPOT, daybeds are the space-saver of choice for many of today's smaller interiors. This French antique piece is the focal point of the room, surrounded by all-but-invisible furnishings such as the sheer curtains and glass-top table.

◄ A PAIR OF DAYBEDS forms an L-shaped sectional in this sitting room, made more comfortable by bolsters and assorted pillows. Both the pillows and the gold spreads can quickly be put away when overnight guests arrive; the twin bed arrangement can sometimes be more practical than one larger bed.

Deciphering Thread Counts

THREAD COUNT REFERS TO THE NUMBER OF THREADS woven into a 1-in. square of fabric. Plus, the thread count will tell you whether a sheet is muslin or percale. Sheets that have a thread count between 140 and 180 are generally considered muslin, whereas sheets with a count higher than 180 are percale. The majority of today's sheets are percale, falling into the 200 to 250 range. You will find some, however, that go as high as 300 to 400. Not surprisingly, these sheets—silky to the touch—are the most luxurious and the most expensive. The bottom line is this: The higher the thread count, the softer the sheets and the more expensive they'll be.

HEADBOARDS

▶ ARCHITECTURE-INSPIRED DESIGNS
are a welcome addition in rooms that
lack built-in interest. In this space,
headboards have the look of wood
paneling, accented with posts and
finials on either side. The vertical lines
of the headboards echo the wallpaper
stripes, tying the pieces to the room.

▼ CARVED FLORAL MOTIFS in these headboards inspired the bed coverings and the
matching window treatment, which convey
a feminine feeling. To make this room
more gender neutral, the floral print linens
could be exchanged for some in solid red
or green hues.

Picking the Perfect Pillow

JUST LIKE CHOOSING A MATTRESS, picking the
right pillow is a matter of personal preference. Pillows filled with feathers or
down are the most comfortable (feathers
offer more support but down is softer). Both,
however, will last as long as 10 years. There
are plenty of synthetic- and polyester-filled
pillows on the market, as well. Some are less
expensive than those with a natural fill but
they don't wear as well. On the other hand,
memory foam pillows, which conform to the
contour of your head and neck, are compara-
ble in price—and quality—to natural-fill pillows. Finally, there are solutions for those
with allergies, too. Hypoallergenic pillows
are readily available as are pillow casings
that prevent dust mites from penetrating.

▲ RUGS CAN BE IDEAL STARTING POINTS for color schemes. Here, colors throughout the room can all be traced back to the floor covering, including the creamy white of the headboard. Its wraparound style provides just enough curves to soften the geometry of the rug.

BUNK BEDS

▲ YOU DON'T HAVE TO POSITION BUNK BEDS one on top of the other. This L-shaped configuration incorporates storage drawers beneath the bottom bunk and each bed has its own a display niche. Safety rails are made out of common pipes, and recessed lights mean no bumping your head on a fixture.

◄ THESE MIRROR-IMAGE SLEEPING SPOTS feature lower bunks set in blue laminate-covered frames that incorporate storage at the foot of each bed. Because they are higher than average, they need safety railings just like the mattresses in the loft—a cool place to have sleepovers.

Built-in Beds

BUILT-IN BEDS WERE ORIGINALLY CONCEIVED IN COOLER CLIMATES, where their cocoon-like atmospheres provided another level of warmth, both from a literal point of view and psychologically, too. With today's improved heating systems, the former isn't as important anymore but the latter reason remains intact. Even if a built-in is added for a purely practical purpose, the result is inevitably cozy comfort. That's especially so when, in true Scandinavian style, a decorative facade creates a cubbyhole-like entrance, making the bed even more of a retreat. The only downside is that the bed can be a bit more difficult to make in the morning, but it's a small price to pay for the sense of security that it provides. Another advantage of built-in beds is that you can add built-in storage, too. Drawers set into the base of a bed can store everything from extra blankets to off-season clothing.

► A CARVED FACADE creates a cozy niche in this guest room, giving you a sense of peering into a secret hideaway. With the fun comes function, however; each bed has four drawers built conveniently into the foot.

Desks

EVERYONE NEEDS A DESK OF SOME SORT, whether it's for paying bills, catching up on correspondence, or running a home-based business. At one extreme, slim writing tables can slip into the living room, family room, even the bedroom. Their diminutive size is by no means a reflection of how hard they work, either; they are good candidates for double duty, whether it's as a casual serving spot or as a bedside table.

Secretaries, roll-tops, and drop-lid desks come with myriad compartments and cubbyholes, making them good choices for those who like to take organization to the *n*th degree. No matter what kind of desk you opt for, be sure that it has sufficient lighting and is located close to a power source. In this age of technology, every desk is sure to accommodate a computer—even a laptop—at some point in time.

▲ A DESK THAT'S FINISHED ON ALL FOUR SIDES is a perfect candidate to "float" within a room. By pulling this desk away from the wall and locating it in front of a floor-to-ceiling built-in, the owners created a home office in a sliver of space.

▲ POSITIONED AT A RIGHT ANGLE to a window, this desk gets plenty of natural light, a plus in any home office. The windows and French doors are dressed in an off-white hue, the same shade used on a pair of chairs. Neutral colors like these are conducive to quiet contemplation.

Built-in Desks

REAL SPACE SAVERS in today's smaller homes, built-in desks have become commonplace in the kitchen, providing a place to pay bills, make out grocery lists, and even supervise the kids while they're doing homework. The concept has worked so well, in fact, that built-in desks have now moved beyond the kitchen, showing up almost anywhere throughout the house. In some cases, mere slivers of space are being transformed into handy home offices.

An underused closet, for instance, can be converted into an office area, with storage space reaching all the way to the ceiling. Plus, when unexpected guests arrive, you can simply close the door on the clutter. A slim desk can be built in under a window, too, taking advantage of the natural light. You can add a matching bench that can tuck under the work surface or simply keep a lightweight chair nearby that can be pulled up as needed.

▲ A U-SHAPED CONFIGURATION in this narrow space is the epitome of efficiency. The unit wraps around to provide a place for a computer as well as floor-to-ceiling storage. The skirted chair is on casters, so moving across the hardwood floor as work requires is easy.

▶ THIS CONTEMPORARY BUILT-IN DESK features an elongated arched surface with aluminum trim, a design matched exactly in the accompanying bench. A simple folding screen to one side creates a sense of privacy, dividing this minimal home office from the living room beyond.

SECRETARIES AND DROP-LID DESKS

▲ DROP-LID DESKS CAN PROVIDE A WORK SURFACE at a moment's notice. And, when unexpected guests arrive, you can quickly close the lid on the clutter immediately. The plaid chair serves double-duty for both the desk and the room.

▲ THE FRENCH SECRÉTAIRE, with a vertical drop lid, dates back more than three centuries. It gets a modern translation, however, in this painted version. More formal in style than its English slant-top counterpart, it's a particularly good fit for a living room or master bedroom.

▲ THIS SECRETARY is so highly decorative that its work purpose seems almost secondary. It features chinoiserie painting; dating back to early Far Eastern trading, the art form typically features everything from pagodas and people to exotic birds and flowers.

Reproductions vs. Adaptations

W HEN SHOPPING FOR FURNITURE, **particularly pieces that are rich in tradition, it's important to know the difference between reproductions and adaptations. A reproduction is a copy of a fine antique piece; it can be a mirror image right down to the way it's constructed or simply be a line-for-line replica on the outside. Adaptations, on the other hand, slightly alter the original design to better suit today's lifestyles. In the case of an armoire, for instance, it may be tall and deeper in order to house modern electronics. Likewise, four-poster beds are more often adaptations rather than reproductions; when first designed in the eighteenth century, king- and queen-size beds were unheard of.**

WRITING TABLES

▼ RECYCLING IS AT ITS BEST in this study spot, where a reclaimed work surface is supported by an old file cabinet and stacking drawers on one end and a pair of columns on the other. All are painted the same charcoal gray to disguise their various ages and provide continuity.

▲ A SIMPLE WRITING TABLE and slat-back chair, both in a chocolate brown finish, are aptly suited for this masculine room. Against much lighter walls, the furniture is silhouetted beautifully and conveys a sense of serenity at the same time.

Storage Solutions

SMART STORAGE IS MORE ABOUT CREATIVITY than how much money you spend. Here are just a few ideas that anyone can incorporate:

- Add convenient storage to the backs of doors in the form of hooks and racks.
- Use a decorative screen to create a two-sided storage wall. Add clothes hooks on one side and stack storage bins against the other.
- Use baskets to organize specific items, including everything from kids' toys to office supplies.

▲ TUCKED INTO A NICHE that looks as if it were custom built for this piece of furniture, a cream-colored writing table takes a back seat, design-wise, to the more decorative chair. The desk surface has just enough room for the essentials—a laptop, a lamp, and a hot cup of coffee.

4

Room Arrangements

Coming up with a good room arrangement may seem daunting. It doesn't have to be, however, if you take the process step by step. Begin by making a sketch of the room, including its size, shape, and dimensions. And refer to it while you're shopping because furniture often appears smaller in a spacious showroom than it does at home. Next, make a list of your wants and needs, taking into consideration every member of the family. While you may want a quiet reading corner in the family room, there may be a greater need for a family computer to occupy that space.

Once the priorities of the room have been established, play with the possibilities. But don't settle quickly on the first solution. Instead, try several alternatives. That way, you're more likely to come up with the best arrangement for your family. There's often more than one good choice so file your second option away for future use. If you grow tired of the first floor plan, your back-up plan will give you—and your furniture—a fresh outlook.

◄ DIVIDING A ROOM INTO TWO SEPARATE AREAS can be achieved in a number of ways. This combination living and dining area is defined first by the flooring—the former gets an area rug while the latter does not. The two spaces also take an opposite approach to color.

The Entry

I N TERMS OF ROOM ARRANGEMENTS, the entry often gets overlooked. In fact, it should be one of your first considerations. After all, your entry makes a first impression on your guests. But it needs to be just as functional as it is fashionable. It should direct traffic, steering people along the proper routes without any furniture getting in the way. A round table centered in an entry, for instance, might naturally direct visitors to one doorway or another, but only if there is sufficient space to get by it. If you have to squeeze around it on either side, the dramatic impact quickly loses it effect. Instead, you might opt for a slim console table along one wall, letting an area rug direct traffic to the doorways beyond. Even though the entry can be small, the floor plan possibilities are not.

▼ THE RUG IN THIS SPACE leads the eye directly to a niche directly opposite the front door, featuring an angular table custom-made for the architectural bay. Its careful placement keeps the table out of the area's traffic pattern.

▲ IN THIS ENTRYWAY, a hefty Dutch door calls for furnishings that balance its visual weight. An antique table is up to the task; also crafted of dark, rich wood, it's extra long, providing tabletop space for eclectic accessories that give a hint of the home's overall style.

▲ JUST LIKE OTHER ROOMS IN YOUR HOME, the entry should feature a focal point. Here, a geometric-patterned rug draws attention and establishes a contemporary tone. The floor covering aligns with the room's console table and bench, giving each piece more importance.

WHY THIS ENTRY WORKS

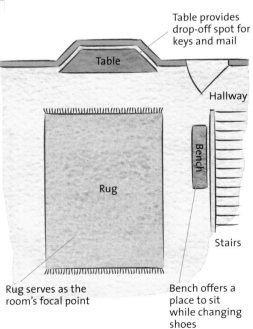

Table provides drop-off spot for keys and mail

Table

Hallway

Bench

Rug

Stairs

Rug serves as the room's focal point

Bench offers a place to sit while changing shoes

Flooring with the Right Stuff

▼ AN OPEN FLOOR PLAN requires creating the sense of an entry. To accomplish that you need little more than a few key pieces of furniture. Here, a central table invites guests to pause once inside the door. A full-length mirror provides a place for a last-minute appearance check.

B Y IT'S VERY NATURE, the foyer is one of the most highly trafficked rooms in the house. Therefore, it's important to choose flooring that's up to the task. One of the most popular options is hardwood, or you might choose a less-expensive laminate that mimics the look of the real thing. Another is tile, ranging from glossy ceramics to terra cottas with subtle matte finishes. The beauty of all these choices is more than skin deep, too; all lend themselves to being topped with area rugs that can bring color and softness to the space.

◄ TO VISUALLY BALANCE THE STAIRWAY on one side of this entry, a chest is set on the other side. So that the overall design doesn't appear too angular, a mirror with a graceful arch is hung on the wall.

▼ IN THIS ENTRY, a decorative chest takes its color cue from the dramatic double doors—right down to the gold trim. An equally elaborate mirror reflects the light coming through the glass-fronted doors, and a pair of sconces and lighting above the crown molding provides nighttime illumination.

TRICKS OF THE TRADE

Putting It on Paper

THERE'S AN EASIER WAY TO FIGURE A ROOM ARRANGEMENT than pushing furniture around. Put your plans on paper first. Measure your room and sketch it onto a piece of ¼-in. grid paper. Include features such as windows and doors, electrical outlets, and architectural elements such as fireplaces. Next, measure the furniture that you plan to use and make templates that are also on a ¼-in.-scale. Draw them on plain white paper so it's easy to see them against the gridded floor plan. Make several copies, and then cut them out, arranging them on your floor plan until you find a look you like. If you prefer not to start from scratch, purchase ready-to-trace furniture templates or room-planning kits at your local art or office supply store.

Coming and Going with Ease: The Bare Necessities

THERE ARE CERTAIN BASICS THAT EVERY ENTRY NEEDS. Before you walk out the door, chances are you'll want a last-minute check of your appearance. A mirror will fulfill that need and also reflect more light into what can be a dark space. When you return home, you'll want a drop-off spot for keys and mail; put a table or chest beneath the wall-hung mirror and you have an instant focal point for the room. Finally, set a chair or bench in your entry. You'll use it to sit down and change shoes or boots.

▲ A WINE BARREL-TURNED-PLANTER takes center stage in this entry. Its round shape mimics the room's curved architecture as well as the circular pendant fixture. An Oriental runner visually balances the curved edges while underscoring the one-of-a-kind piece of furniture in the process.

▶ SET IN THE CENTER of this entry, a table makes a striking statement. Similar in color to the hardwood floor, the piece would have become visually lost without the contrasting rug, which redefines the table's shape and curvaceous legs.

▲ ANCHORED BY A SIMPLE PINE TABLE, this entry is practical and appealing. A pair of drawers is available for stashing small items, and baskets on the shelf below are convenient for storing outdoor gear. A trio of botanical prints breaks up the table's two-by-two symmetry and brings the outdoors in.

The Family Room

CREATING A SUCCESSFUL ARRANGEMENT IN THE FAMILY ROOM may be the easiest of all. Simply start with your largest seating piece, the sofa, and orient it toward the room's focal point, typically the home-entertainment center. More often than not, this multipurpose storage piece is best placed against the largest wall. Complete the seating group, making sure that each piece of furniture is no more than 8 ft. to 10 ft. apart for easy conversation. Because you should be able to view the television without craning your neck, swivel chairs are often a good solution. Also keep in mind that this is the place where casual meals are regularly served. Sit in each seat, making sure that there's a nearby place to set a glass or dish. If not, you'll need to add a small table or two.

▲ A SIMPLE PILLOW can adjust a seating piece to almost any comfort level. This one has a decorative purpose, too, breaking up a solid neutral scheme with a striped pattern.

▲ IN A FAMILY ROOM, where comfort is required, an ottoman often makes more sense than a conventional coffee table. This one, which introduces a soft green hue into the neutral color scheme, has a tightly upholstered top, making it easy to set down a tray of beverages or a stack of books.

▲ OPPOSITE THE SOFA, a pair of leather club chairs can be part of the main grouping or provide a place for one-on-one conversation. Flanking a small table with a reading lamp, the large chairs are ideal for curling up with a good book, too.

▲ A PAIR OF CORNER WINDOWS seemed to inspire the L-shaped configuration of this conversation area. The sofa takes its place along the long wall, and the matching chair is set at a right angle, leaving room for an end table to tuck neatly between the two.

That's Entertainment

L ET'S FACE IT: In most family rooms, the television is a prized possession. Therefore, it needs to be given a place of prominence in the room. You may opt for a custom built-in unit, one that has specific spaces not only for the TV but also CD and DVD players. These units can consist of open shelving, so that the electronics are readily available 24/7. On the other hand, you may want to incorporate doors so that they're hidden from view when not in use. Likewise, there's a wide variety of freestanding furniture available today. You'll find everything from impressive armoires to chests that, with a simple click of the remote, reveal flat-screen TVs.

WHY THIS FAMILY ROOM WORKS

An ottoman does double-duty, providing a tablelike surface and extra seating.

Seating pieces are no more than 10 ft. apart, allowing for easy conversation.

Art

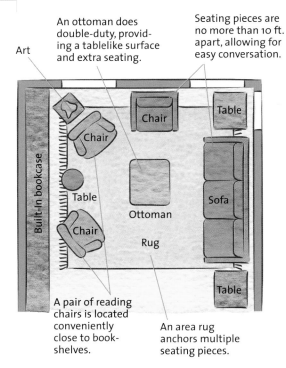

A pair of reading chairs is located conveniently close to book-shelves.

An area rug anchors multiple seating pieces.

▲ THE CIRCULAR FURNITURE ARRANGE-
MENT in this family room makes a clear
distinction between living and dining
areas. Instead of the conventional arrangement of a sofa and two chairs, this seating
group includes a loveseat and three chairs,
all set at an angle for easy conversation.

High-Low Tables

TODAY'S FAMILY ROOMS ARE MULTIFUNCTIONAL, accommodating everything
from casual conversation and TV viewing to homework and even
the occasional meal. It makes sense, then, to purchase furniture
accordingly. High-low tables, for instance, meet a variety of needs. In the
"low" position they look like and act like any other wooden coffee table.
A simple lift of the tabletop, though, raises its height, making it just
right for dining, homework, or table games. Some models are even set
on casters, allowing this flexible piece of furniture to be moved anywhere in the room.

▶ SET AT A RIGHT ANGLE to the stone fireplace, this sofa takes advantage of the fireside view as well as the one beyond the windows. A pair of club chairs complete the grouping; they're angled slightly to allow one to appreciate both vistas.

▼ AN ORIENTAL RUG defines the main conversation area in this family room. In back of the sofa, a drop-leaf table serves two purposes: It provides a place for a reading lamp plus its outer leaf raises, turning the table into a convenient work station.

Kid-Friendly Furnishings

YOU CAN DECORATE WITH KIDS IN MIND and nobody will be the wiser: Today's most durable furnishings don't sacrifice style. For children still in the crawling stages, use soft rugs and carpets. Natural fibers such as cotton and wool are good choices, plus they give off fewer VOCs (volatile organic compounds) than synthetic fibers. Likewise, in the kitchen, use vinyl flooring that has the look of ceramic tile but provides a softer landing for toddlers just beginning to walk. For kids of all ages, though, use washable fabrics or fit seating pieces with slipcovers that you can toss in the wash.

▼ A PLUSH SOFA anchors this seating group, its color inspired by the brick fireplace surround. The warm hue is repeated on the piping of the companion chair. Tying all of the furniture together is an area rug; its band of colors leads the eye from one piece to the other.

▲ WHEN A CONVERSATION GROUPING floats in the middle of a room, as it often does in an open floor plan, it's important to solidly anchor it. That happens here with the help of a solid-color sofa and chairs and a lime-stone-topped table for good measure.

◄ BORN OF NECESSITY, this built-in television cabinet provides a focal point, too. Simple furnishings focus on the unit, gathering around an oversize wicker ottoman that provides put-your-feet-up comfort as well as additional seating.

The Great Room

A GREAT ROOM LITERALLY DOES IT ALL, providing living and dining areas while opening up to a kitchen on one side of the space. All that room can seem luxurious but, at the same time, can provide a challenge in terms of furniture arrangements. There are, after all, few walls against which pieces can be placed. Floating arrangements work best in this case, with large pieces such as sofas serving as room dividers. It's particularly important in great rooms, to plot out your room arrangement on paper first. Determine the placement not only of major pieces but also of each table, each rug, and each lamp. Once the lighting is in place, have an electrician add floor outlets where necessary to eliminate cords that can be tripped on.

▼ THIS GREAT ROOM PROVIDES THE LUXURY of not one but two living areas in addition to dining space. The red sofa and the console table behind it serve as a room divider, separating the conversation area from the dining area beyond. The sofa's bright color further emphasizes the division.

◄ A CURVED EDGE on this island makes for a more intimate kitchen eating area. But it has a practical purpose, too. The shaved-away edge keeps the island from jutting too far into the adjacent space, which, in turn, would interrupt the traffic flow.

▼ THE VIEW FROM THE KITCHEN to the secondary sitting area conveys the significant role that neutrals play in this space, running the gamut from bright white to charcoal gray. It's important in a great room to keep accent colors consistent; this shade of red visually connects each separate area.

WHY THIS GREAT ROOM WORKS

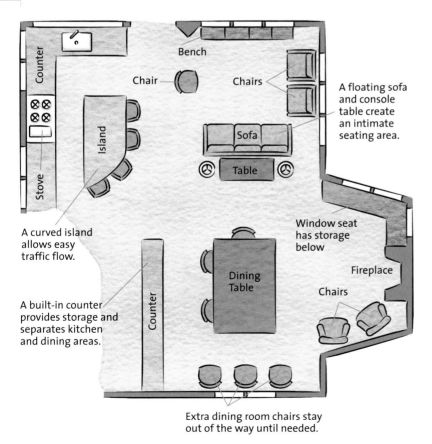

Bench

Chair

Chairs

Chairs

A floating sofa and console table create an intimate seating area.

Sofa

Counter

Island

Stove

Table

A curved island allows easy traffic flow.

Window seat has storage below

Fireplace

A built-in counter provides storage and separates kitchen and dining areas.

Counter

Dining Table

Chairs

Extra dining room chairs stay out of the way until needed.

▲ A SOFT GRAY SOFA anchors one end
of this great room. It's the area rug,
however, that defines the conversation
space, allowing the much-darker
coffee table to remain the center of
attention. The table's square shape
echoes the windows around the room.

◄ CONTRASTING TONES are important
in any neutral color scheme because
they create visual interest. In this case,
the black and neutral combination
allows the shapes of the slat-back
chairs and simple table to stand out
more distinctly.

Open Floor Plans: Creating Continuity

B Y ITS VERY NATURE, a great room opens up to at least one other room, typically the kitchen, and sometimes more. So when planning the color palette, you have to take those rooms into consideration, too. Once you've settled on your scheme, look for ways to work one or two of the hues into the adjoining areas. The upholstery fabric on the great room sofa might reappear on the seats of your counter stools or the paint color that you choose may also find its way onto the cabinet trim. Even small touches will go a long way in achieving a cohesive plan.

▼ A SOFA OFTEN SERVES as a room divider but here a pair of side-by-side chairs serves the same purpose. Because they are placed close together, the chairs convey the same visual effect as a single, larger piece.

▼ IN THIS GREAT ROOM, the center of attention is a soaring two-story fireplace. Painted a golden yellow to give it even greater focus, the angular architectural element is countered by the soft curves of the nearby sofa and chairs.

▲ HERE, THE VIEW FROM THE DINING AREA to the front door includes the living area on the right side and a kitchen on the left. To mark the spot where you can see throughout the entire level, a boxed star is inlaid into the hardwood floor.

▲ AN OPEN FLOOR PLAN with a great room is casual by nature. That relaxed attitude is carried out in the kitchen where one end of the counter is raised, providing a place to share a glass of wine or converse with the cook.

Rhythm

RHYTHM ISN'T JUST IMPORTANT IN MUSICAL TERMS; it's equally crucial to a well-orchestrated room. Visual rhythm flows throughout a room, leading the eye from one design element to the next. You can, for instance, create rhythm with a dominant pattern. A large-scale floral might appear first on the sofa, again on a window treatment and, finally, on a few decorative pillows. The result is a soft, gradual flow, much like a ballad. A more contemporary room, on the other hand, is apt to have a jazzier style, the space punctuated with bright splashes of color.

You can also create the same effect with textures. Intersperse a neutral room with eye-catching textures that keep the eye moving from place to place. A shag rug and a rough-hewn beam will quickly add visual interest. It does not matter what kind of design element you use—color, pattern, texture, even groups of treasured collectibles—as long as you keep the eye moving from one point of interest to another.

▲ THE PREDOMINANT SQUARE MOTIF of the built-in storage in this room is repeated throughout, appearing on seat cushions, decorative pillows, the sofa's arms, and even the mullioned windows. The result? A rhythm that's instantly relaxing.

The Living Room

THERE ARE NO HARD AND FAST RULES in terms of room arrangements, even in the living room. But a few guidelines will help you create a comfortable and inviting atmosphere. When placing your main seating pieces, keep in mind that people are most at ease sitting across from each other or at right angles. It's hard to converse if you're sitting too closely together side by side; even if your sofa can feasibly accommodate four people, plan on seating no more than three. For additional seating, use benches, ottomans, and nearby dining room chairs. Small upholstered cubes are a good choice, too. When not in use, they can tuck away under a console table. Some cocktail tables even come with cubes that nest underneath the tabletop until they're needed.

Once you've lived with your furniture plan for a while reassess how it's working. If it feels like you have too much furniture, don't hesitate to move a piece or two to another room. It's all part of finding the right comfort level.

▶ IN ROOMS THAT SEE A LOT OF ENTERTAINING, lightweight and portable seating pieces are necessary. Here, a slipcovered armchair and its armless counterpart can be easily moved by guests, allowing them to join a group gathering or a more intimate conversation.

▼ A LAMP ON THIS SKIRTED END TABLE would have meant a long electrical cord running to the wall outlet. Because that's not only unsightly but also unsafe, a pair of small lamps was set atop the nearby bookcase, casting soft ambient light on the space.

WHY THIS LIVING ROOM WORKS

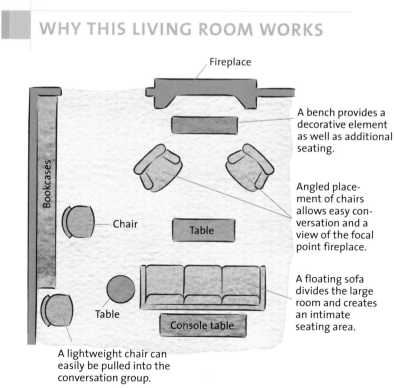

Fireplace

A bench provides a decorative element as well as additional seating.

Angled placement of chairs allows easy conversation and a view of the focal point fireplace.

A floating sofa divides the large room and creates an intimate seating area.

Bookcases

Chair

Table

Table

Console table

A lightweight chair can easily be pulled into the conversation group.

▲ COVERING BOTH SOFAS IN THE SAME FLORAL FABRIC would have created too much visual weight for this pale-painted room. To avoid that, one sofa is upholstered in pale blue floral fabric and the other is covered in a solid cream color. Armchairs in both fabrics create a relaxing sense of rhythm.

Managing Traffic Flow

WHEN PLANNING A ROOM arrangement, be sure to create an easy traffic flow. Check, for instance, that people don't have to walk through a major seating group in order to get from one room to another. Instead, position your furniture so it directs traffic around the area, so conversations aren't interrupted. Note that traffic lanes should be at least 3 ft. wide to allow people to pass through easily.

▲ A PAIR OF CURVED SECTIONALS provides a welcome counterpoint in a room full of straight edges, including the beamed ceiling, the stone fireplace, and the strip hardwood flooring. Teamed with a round cocktail table and circular rug, the seating pieces soften a potentially too-rigid space.

◄ SOME PIECES OF FURNITURE can define a conversation area just as well as a rug. In the living area of this open floor plan, a pair of corner chairs is strategically placed along one side. Their squared-off forms leave no question as to the boundaries of this grouping.

▶ A DIAGONAL ROOM ARRANGEMENT can often be very inviting, allowing easy access into a major conversation group. That's the case in this living room, where an L-shaped sofa has a good view of the fireplace while "pointing out" the impressive window wall.

▼ FOUR UPHOLSTERED CHAIRS provide individual comfort as well as easy conversation in this living area, giving the dark paneled room a more open and airy feeling. The central table serves them all, too, so there's no need for extraneous side tables that would have hindered access to the sitting spot.

Finding Focal Points

EVEN IF YOU KNOW PRECISELY WHICH SEATING PIECES you want to use in a room, there's still the question of where to put them. By looking around, you'll usually find a clue. The main conversation group should be oriented toward a focal point, an object or architectural element that's pleasing to view. A fireplace is a natural focal point as is a grand Palladian window that looks out onto a beautiful view. But even if your room has no architectural assets, there are still plenty of options. An impressive work of art is one possibility. Or look to a more practical piece of furniture. A striking storage piece, such as an armoire, can attract attention while fulfilling its utilitarian purpose. By outfitting it with home entertainment equipment, including a television set, you can accomplish two things at once. With the doors closed, it serves as decorative focal point. Open the doors, however, and it's perfectly placed for easy TV viewing.

▶ A FIREPLACE is a natural focal point for any room. The importance of this one is emphasized, though, with the addition of an eye-catching mirror directly above it. The round mirror is also a welcome change from the more angular fireplace as well as the windows on either side.

▲ CREAMY WHITE SOFAS in this L-shape arrangement allow occupants to view a cozy fire or admire the view through grand Palladian windows. Just as important is their neutral hue; it, with the room's bright white ceiling and trim, provides visual relief from the brilliant red walls.

The Dining Room

THE BEST DINING ROOMS are those that make you want to linger over coffee and dessert. But creating a comfortable space requires more than just buying a quality table and chairs. First, choose a table that's well made and spacious enough. To give each diner enough room, allow 24 in. to 30 in. for each place setting. In terms of chairs, armless styles fit under tables more easily than those with arms, but armchairs provide a place to rest your elbows. If you opt for armchairs, they should slide completely under the table so be sure to measure carefully. Just because an armchair is shorter than the tabletop doesn't necessarily mean it will slide underneath; many tables have aprons (skirt-like bands of wood under the tabletop) that prevent pushing in chairs more than an inch or two. Keep in mind, too, that chairs with backs high enough to support your head are the most comfortable.

▼ SET ON AN AREA RUG, a pedestal table and four upholstered chairs are the undisputed focal point in this room. When a buffet meal is served, the checked chairs pull back to join their striped counterparts around the room's perimeter, allowing the table to be transformed into a serving station.

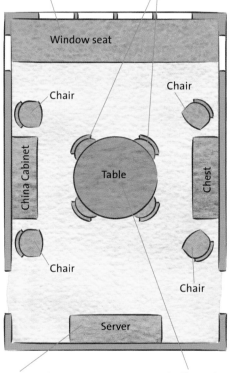

Teamed with a small table, the windowseat can serve as a secondary dining area.

Angled placement of chairs allows more pass-through room between them and the surrounding furnishings.

Window seat

Chair

Chair

China Cabinet

Chair

Table

Chest

Chair

Chair

Server

A server doubles as a writing desk.

For buffet-style meals, dining chairs move to the perimeter of the room and the table becomes a serving station.

▲ MORE AND MORE ROOMS are taking on extra jobs today, providing various functions. Here, a slim table can serve up appetizers and drinks. On a daily basis, though, it is a handy writing desk. The nearby dining chair pulls up to provide seating.

▲ THIS DINING ROOM ARRANGEMENT COULDN'T BE MORE BASIC—eight chairs surrounding a rectangular table. It goes from ordinary to extraordinary, though, with the jet-black chairs silhouetted against the white surround, including the dining table and a slim console. Two more chairs pull up whenever the table's leaf is added.

▲ FOR SMALL SPACES, square dining tables—just big enough to seat four—are becoming a popular choice. This table is teamed with upholstered chairs that have the option of two different looks, with or without the apron-style slipcovers that complement the striped upholstery.

Visual Weight

VISUAL WEIGHT can't be measured by scales; instead, it's all about perception. An overstuffed armchair, for instance, has more visual weight than its small wicker counterpart. Likewise, a table made of wood appears heavier than one of glass. Even if two objects are exactly the same size and shape, one can appear weightier from a visual point of view. A sofa upholstered in a large-scale floral print appears more overpowering than the same style in a small check. Similarly, one in a dark, solid color has more visual weight than one covered in light neutral hue. It's all part of the balancing act that adds up to a well-designed room.

◄ THERE'S A STRONG RHYTHM in this room, due to the repetition of rectangular shapes, showing up in the dining table, the chairs, the rug, and even the light fixture. The latter is a particularly good choice; because it echoes the shape of the table, the entire surface is lit evenly.

◀ THIS SIMPLE SPACE needs nothing more than the architecture to define it clearly; the niche is a natural spot for a casual dining area. Chairs that are light in color and weight can be easily pulled into the nearby conversation area on a moment's notice.

▼ ON A DAY-TO-DAY BASIS, this dining room table is surrounded by four wooden chairs, painted to match the room's woodwork. When extra guests need to be accommodated, the table is pulled closer to the nearby blue bench, with the extra chair moving to the opposite side.

▲ THANKS TO THE GLASS-TOP TABLE, arm-chairs in this dining room have a sculptural quality that comes through beautifully. Had they not been in a white hue, they may have seemed too heavy for the room. As is, they blend wonderfully with the backdrop, con-trasted only by the rough-hewn wood server.

Shaping Up Dining Space

T O DETERMINE WHAT SHAPE YOUR DINING TABLE SHOULD BE, **look first** at the room itself. If it's on the square side, consider a table that's square, too. If you need to allow room for a china cabinet or sideboard at one end or the other, you may even want to use a drop-leaf table. Similarly, a rectangular room calls for a table that replicates the room's shape. If space is on the tight side, choose an oval shape that shaves just a little off the corners.

The Bedroom

ODAY'S BEDROOMS ARE MORE THAN SLEEPING SPOTS—they're multi-purpose spaces. It's not unusual for a bedroom to include a reading corner, a place to watch TV, or even a home office area. Because it serves so many functions, it's important to plan the room arrangement by zones. That doesn't mean that the bed has to be banished to a corner, but home office areas and, to an even greater extent, seating groups that include TVs, should be situated so they can be used without disturbing someone who wishes to sleep.

In addition, there are some practical matters to take into account when planning a bedroom. Be sure to allow enough room to make the bed, a minimum of 2 ft. on each side. Likewise, provide at least 36 in. of space in front of a chest so that drawers can be pulled out easily.

▲ IN THIS ROOM, the only available space for the bed is between the window and the slanted ceiling, dictating that the desk be placed on the opposite side. The arrangement works well, though, still allowing plenty of room to make the bed and pull out the desk chair when necessary.

◀ IN A ROOM WITH MINIMAL ARCHITECTURAL ASSETS, furniture takes on more importance. This bed, reminiscent of wood paneling, takes advantage of the garden view. A blue and white striped rug, positioned crossways at the end of the bed, ties the bed to the chair and also brings together the entire color scheme.

WHY THIS BEDROOM WORKS

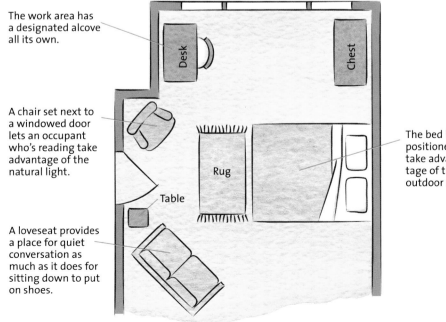

The work area has a designated alcove all its own.

A chair set next to a windowed door lets an occupant who's reading take advantage of the natural light.

A loveseat provides a place for quiet conversation as much as it does for sitting down to put on shoes.

Desk

Chest

Rug

Table

The bed is positioned to take advantage of the outdoor view.

▲ A CANOPY BED is a good choice for a room with a dramatic, vaulted ceiling. One with a shorter, standard headboard would have been too similar in height to the rest of the room's furnishings, visually cutting the room in half horizontally.

▲ IF THERE'S NOT ROOM FOR A BENCH at the foot of the bed and a separate sitting area, combine the two concepts. This chaise fills in nicely for a standard bench while anchoring a seating group that also includes an upholstered armchair. An oversize mirror makes the room appear larger.

◄ THE BENCH AT THE FOOT
OF THIS BED does its part to
add color to the primarily
neutral room, providing a
visual anchor for the bed
in the process. Made of
wicker, like the nearby chair,
it creates a sense of design
continuity, too.

ELEMENTS OF DESIGN

Proportion

ONE OF THE MOST IMPORTANT ASPECTS of any well-planned room is a good sense of proportion. A table should be in proportion to the bed it is next to and the lamp, in turn, should be in proportion to the table it's on. A few furnishings take the guesswork out of it; you'll find lampshades sold separately from their bases but with tags indicating which shade is appropriate for what base. For the most part, though, it's up to you to decide if the relationship is right among furnishings in a room. Some incorrect pairings are obvious. An end table with spindly legs, for example, is all wrong next to an overstuffed easy chair. A better companion for the chair would be a small chest—about the height of the chair's arm.

In the same way, proportion is important when it comes to pattern. A mini-print will get lost on a window treatment that has a long six-ft. span but a large-scale floral is just the right size. The same concept also applies to walls. Reserve wallpapers with big patterns and prints for bedrooms with expansive spaces.

▲ THE GENEROUS SIZE OF THIS BED requires bedside items that are a match proportionally. On either side, twin tables don't appear all that large but, when coupled with the lamps, the effect is well balanced, with much of the credit going to the sizeable shades.

▲ A BUMPED-OUT WALL serves as a framework for the gracefully shaped headboard of this bed. With this bed, the mood of the room could have been clearly formal but the blue and white checked upholstery takes it into the realm of casually elegant.

Be My Guest

THERE'S MORE TO A RELAXING GUEST ROOM than a comfortable bed. Provide a small chest of drawers, empty and ready for your guests to use, as well as some hanging space in the closet. If there's room, add a cozy reading spot that includes a comfortable chair, a side table, and a lamp. Finally, a small television, a stack of magazines, an alarm clock, bottled water, plus a bowl of fruit or fresh flowers will put your hospitality on the same level as a fine hotel. See if your efforts pass the test by spending a night there yourself.

▼ INSTEAD OF MATCHING NIGHTSTANDS, multifunctional furnishings are used in this bedroom. On one side of the bed is a group of nesting tables; the top one accommodates bedside necessities while the other two can be moved around the room as needed. On the other side, a writing desk serves double-duty.

▲ THE RIGHT FURNISHINGS can create a greater sense of height in a room. The floral-strewn bed curtains on this metal canopy bed draw the eye almost up to the ceiling while window treatments in the same patterned fabric go all the way to the top.

5

Window Treatments

Window dressings are the hardest-working elements in a decorating scheme. They control light and protect furniture and fabrics from fading. They provide privacy and frame views. They even conserve energy. If you have a bedroom with eastern-facing windows, for example, wooden blinds will keep the sun from waking you before the alarm. In a bathroom with a spectacular view, honeycomb shades will keep things confidential but, when raised, will stack to mere inches so that you can appreciate the vista. Plus they have energy-saving properties, making rooms warmer in winter and cooler in the summer.

As much as they are multifunctional, window treatments are also fashionable. If you're a minimalist, you may choose something as simple as Roman shades. If you're after something more opulent, consider sheer curtains coupled with floor-length draperies and topped with elegant swags and jabots.

The right choice of dressings can also visually change the dimensions of a window. A standard, double-hung style, for instance, can be lengthened with curtains that reach to the floor. To give the same window even more importance, extend the width of the treatment by using a longer rod and adding an extra panel on either side.

◄ WHAT COULD HAVE BEEN VERY ORDINARY CURTAINS in this bedroom are extraordinary, thanks to a decorative rod and lush fabric that puddles generously onto the floor. A floor-to-ceiling shade completes the treatment, making the window seem taller in the process.

Draperies

EOPLE TEND TO DISTINGUISH DRAPERIES FROM CURTAINS by their level of elegance. Draperies are thought to be formal, whereas curtains are assumed to be more appropriate for informal settings. In fact, the differences are more technical. By definition, draperies are pleated panels that hang from hooks attached to a traverse rod. They're opened and closed with a cord that moves the panels and are typically lined and even interlined, making them hang better and more energy efficient.

Curtains, on the other hand, are unlined and opened and closed by hand, not by pulling a cord. Don't think for a minute, though, that they give up anything in terms of style. They're hung from rods in all kinds of creative ways—from those that are softly gathered to others that have more tailored tab tops and button right onto the rod. Even their valances and cornices are simply casual translations of draperies' more formal renditions.

▲ IN THIS BEDROOM, a swag and jabot treatment beautifully frames a double-hung window. The floral fabric and tassel trim are repeated in the nearby bed canopy, tying the window and bed dressings together. Both are more noticeable next to the striped wallpaper than they would have been against a busier pattern.

▼ IN A LIVING ROOM FULL OF TRADITIONAL FLORALS AND PRINTS, a crisp green and white striped window treatment adds contemporary flair. Its cool color balances the warm red plaid chair on the opposite side of the room. The extra-wide stripes are especially well suited to the pleated valance, echoing the vertical lines.

About Window Treatments

- **Swag:** (see p. 164, top right): Made up of sweeping folds of fabric that extend from one corner of a window to the other.
- **Jabot:** (see p. 164, top right): Typically hung on either side of a swag, it falls into deep pleats, and has an angled bottom edge.
- **Valance:** (see p. 164, bottom left): A window topper made of gathered or pleated fabric.
- **Cornice:** (see p. 165, top right): A three sided, upholstered box that tops a window.
- **Roman shade:** (see p. 176, top right): Flat and typically fitted with horizontal dowels that allow it to raise into soft folds.
- **Balloon shade:** (see p. 176, bottom left): Adjusted by cords; as the shade is raised, fullness increases at the bottom.

▲ A NEUTRAL SCHEME, which carries over onto the window treatments, keeps things quiet in this living room. Scalloped cornices in an off-white hue top side panels in the same subtle color; the cornices extend all the way to the ceiling, making the windows seem taller in the process.

◄ A WINDOW TREATMENT CAN SERVE as a secondary headboard for a bed. In this sleeping space, a floral valance and matching drapery panels frame a well-dressed metal bed. Roll-up shades made of bamboo provide privacy, their natural color not competing at all with the more colorful fabric treatment for attention.

► A SCENIC TOILE PATTERN wraps this bedroom, from the window treatments—with elegant pleated and fringed valances—right onto the walls. With so much pattern, it's important to have a resting place for the eye, provided here by simple white bed linens.

▼ SOME KIND OF VISUAL INTEREST is important when draperies blend quietly into the background. These upholstered cornices provide that eye-catching element, their stepped shapes right in line with the understated plaid fabric of the window treatment.

Picking the Right Fabric

WHEN CHOOSING A FABRIC for your window treatments, it's important to understand which ones work best for what styles. Swags, for instance, should drape into soft folds. Conversely, heavy canvas-like fabrics are perfectly suitable for flat curtain panels, upholstered cornices, even Roman shades.

Also take a close look at your pattern of choice. Solid colors and small to medium prints work just about anywhere, but fabrics that repeat large patterns are better used on window treatments that are equally large in scale. To appreciate the design to its fullest, make sure that it doesn't get lost in too many folds of fabrics, either.

All the Trimmings

SOMETIMES ALL IT TAKES TO ENHANCE A WINDOW treatment is the right trim. The term *passementerie* encompasses all manner of tassels, fringe, ribbon, and braid. It's important, though, that passementerie be compatible with its companion fabric. If draperies are dry-clean only, make sure that the trimmings are, too. Likewise, if curtains are machine-washable, make sure that any attached trim can be tossed into the washer.

- **Welting:** A fabric-covered cord that typically ranges in diameter from ¼ in. to 1 in.; with a narrow flange (fabric extension) on one edge, it can be stitched right into a seam.
- **Cording:** A ropelike trim made up of twisted threads.
- **Braid:** a flat trim with two finished edges.
- **Gimp:** A narrow braid with looped or scalloped edges.
- **Fringe:** includes brush fringe, with its densely packed threads, bouillon fringe characterized by twisted strands, as well as loop fringe, ball fringe, and tassel fringe.
- **Bullion fringe:** Characterized by twisted strands as well as loop fringe, ball fringe, and tassel fringe.
- **Tassel:** Frequently handcrafted, it's most often used as a tieback for curtains or draperies.

▲ SOME TRIMMINGS ARE SO IMPRESSIVE that they can stand alone as window treatments. In this sitting area, an off-white bullion fringe dances across the tops of the window walls. The casual treatment is in keeping with the beachlike feeling of the room, right down to the comfortable hammock.

▼ THE COMBINATION OF TWO FABRICS gives this swag-and-jabot window dressing a casual attitude. The plaid component echoes the pattern of the nearby sectional seating but doesn't go so far as to repeat it verbatim; meanwhile, its solid yellow counterpart balances the abundance of geometric pattern.

▼ DRESSED IN A BOLD WHITE ON RED PATTERN, the window in this bedroom commands attention. The curtains can be closed for privacy but, when open, frame both the bed and the windows. A softly swagged valance echoes the curves of the muntins as well as the headboard below.

CURTAINS

▶ SHEER CURTAINS AND A CASUALLY DRAPED SCARF create a romantic ambience that's well suited to a bedroom. Here, a subtle leaf motif on the curtains and pillow shams lends a hint of pattern and color to an otherwise solid neutral scheme. Roman shades, tucked behind the sheer curtains, provide privacy.

▼ PROVING THAT SOMETHING SIMPLE CAN BE SMASHING, red and white toile curtains run the length of this window wall. For continuity's sake, the red hue reappears on bed linens and the chair while a bright blue coverlet, pillow shams, and painted floor keep the red from being over-powering.

▲ CHARACTERIZED BY THEIR RUFFLED TOPS, edges, even tiebacks, Priscilla curtains have made a comeback since they were first popular in the 1950s. Their dainty prettiness is particularly appropriate for cottage-style settings like this one, where furnishings are simple and understated.

Sheer Beauty

SHEERS ARE VERSATILE—in more ways than one. They can be a sunny room's best assets, allowing light to gently filter in. Or they can be the perfect counterpoint to heavier, more lavish draperies. In addition, they've long passed the point of being offered in white only. Today there are a wide variety of pale hues, all in keeping with the light weight of the fabrics themselves. Gauzy cottons, filmy voiles, even see-through laces fall into this diaphanous category. And many of them have subtle patterns, too, ranging from geometric plaids and stripes to those with softer, realistic motifs.

No matter what type of sheers you choose, it's important to keep the styling just as simple as the fabric itself (the fabric's not strong enough to stand up to styles with complex pleats and folds). You'll find sheers in many designs at your local home goods store. Or make your own with materials purchased from a fabric store. Perfectly flat panels, for instance—hemmed on all four sides—might be hung from a thin decorative rod with metal clips. For another look, add oversize grommets along the top edge and suspend the sheers from a rod with ribbon.

▲ SHEERS NEED NOT BE CONVENTIONAL FLOOR-LENGTH CURTAINS. In this boy's bedroom, sheer material—no longer than the width of the windows themselves—is simply draped and gathered at the corners with starfish-style hardware, perfectly suited for the room's beachy theme.

◄ ALTHOUGH AN ARCHED WINDOW can sometimes be a challenge to dress, this is the perfect solution: Simple curtains reach only as high as the top horizontal muntin while swing-away rods let the occupant of this window seat fully appreciate the view beyond.

► THIS GIRL'S ROOM starts with all the trappings of tradition right down to the pink and white floral wallpaper. But a bright plaid window treatment—topped with a balloon shade–style valance—gives it a completely fresh twist.

▼ A WINDOW THAT OPENS INWARD and a radiator directly beneath it both pose challenges. The solution: Frame the window with stationary side panels, then add a Roman shade for privacy. This one, positioned at ceiling level, can be pulled up high enough so that the window's still operable.

► WHEN PRIVACY ISN'T A PRIORITY, there's no need to cover the entire window. Here, softly gathered curtains reach only to the windows' midpoints, allowing light for reading and for planters on each sill, which further enhance the gardenlike feeling of the room.

Customizing Ready-Made Curtains

HERE'S A VIRTUAL WEALTH of ready-made curtains available today. But even if you purchase the most basic style—a solid-color neutral, for instance—you can transform the run of the mill into something remarkable. For example, by adding a decorative ribbon along the side and bottom edges, you'll create a personal look. To do this, position the ribbon the same distance from the edges as its width. If you're using a 2-in.-wide ribbon, it should be placed 2 in. from the curtain's edge. You can turn corners with your ribbon or let each length run right off the edge. Or take a simpler approach and sew a piece of ribbon along the top edge of the curtain, then add matching tie tops at 6-in. intervals. If you're more of an artist than a seamstress, you may opt to stencil or stamp motifs along your curtains' edges, using fabric paint.

There are just as many options when it comes to tiebacks. Instead of using the matching ones that come with your curtains, look for things that will play up a room's personality. In a western-style boy's room you might use bandanas or even horseshoes. In a nursery, opt for children's handkerchiefs with a nursery rhyme theme.

◄ CUSTOMIZING OFF-THE-SHELF CURTAINS to suit a room theme can be done in a matter of minutes with a stencil kit from a local crafts supply store. The simple white panels in this room have been given a one-of-a-kind look with starfish stenciled around the edges.

▶ THIS BLUE AND WHITE CURTAIN PANEL gets a custom touch from satin ribbon that echoes the predominant hue of the window dressing. One strip has simply been sewn across the top with matching tie tops attached directly behind it.

▶ THE KEY TO DRESSING corner windows is to keep things simple so that the hardware doesn't get too cumbersome in the corner itself. Thin wire rods almost invisibly support these sill-length curtains. Because the softly scrolled pattern complements the wall color, however, it blends quietly into the room.

◄ THIS WINDOW TOPPER is a casual translation of a more formal window treatment. Instead of the traditional swag in the center, it features a flat panel of fabric that's gracefully shaped before falling into pleated jabots on each side.

▼ SHEER TIEBACK CURTAINS IN THIS BEDROOM allow the eye to move right past the window treatment to the breathtaking view beyond. The curtains are topped with a scalloped blue and white striped valance that also hides shades for privacy.

TRICKS OF THE TRADE

Decorative Rods

EVEN THOUGH DECORATIVE RODS support window treatments of all kinds, they by no means settle for supporting roles. Instead, they're co-stars more often than not, carefully chosen to complement their fabric counterparts. Metal finishes continue to be popular, including conventional brass and wrought iron, but take a look burnished bronze, brushed nickel, aged pewter, and even copper. You'll find the real metals as well as resin-cast look-alikes, providing the heavy metal look without the weight. For contemporary interiors, wire rods are another option—lightweight curtains are simply attached to a length of wire with decorative clips.

Wooden poles, too, are still a perfectly viable option. Beyond the wide variety of painted and stained rods—even those that look like bamboo—there are also natural alternatives that can be finished to your heart's desire. Keep in mind that, whatever material you choose, finials can make a distinct decorative difference. Some rods come with finials attached, but others give you the option of choosing your own, including everything from scrolls and spears to leaves and flowers, and even colored glass.

▲ PAINTED WITH BLACK AND WHITE STRIPES and given polka-dot finials, this decorative rod perfectly complements the short and sassy window treatment. Originally purchased as an unpainted piece, this kind of rod is inexpensive and can be customized to suit any scheme.

FASHION PLEATS

Not all pleats are created equal.

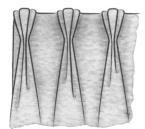

PINCH

A pinch pleat is the most traditional pleat type, made up of a loop of fabric that's folded into three shallow pleats and tacked at the base.

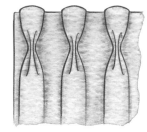

GOBLET

A goblet pleat is formed by tucking the loop of fabric at the base instead of folding it, creating a cylinder in the process; it's appropriate for formal window treatments.

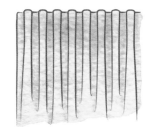

PENCIL

A pencil pleat consists of a small loop that is neither folded nor cinched. It's created with pleating tape sewn to the back of the drapery panel.

BOX

A box pleat is a deep, inverted pleat. This style—suitable only for stationary panels—requires firm support.

▲ A FLAT PIECE OF FABRIC takes on new dimension in this window bay. Attached to the rod by decorative rings, the window treatment is gathered irregularly to give it a more casual flair. In keeping with the informal feeling, the fabric simply falls into angular folds at each end.

◀ STRIPED VALANCES repeat the vertical lines of the beadboard walls in this simple blue and white bathroom with a distinct masculine flair. Suspended by decorative wrought-iron rods, the window treatments cover up shades that pull down for privacy.

▶ A LACEY SHADE adds a touch of softness to this kitchen window, its cut-out pattern allowing light to gently filter in. Meanwhile, a vintage tablecloth creates a unique valance and provides a splash of color.

Sew it Goes

YOU DON'T HAVE TO BE AN ACCOMPLISHED SEAM-STRESS to create stylish toppers for your windows. Without ever threading a needle, you can fashion these in practically no time at all:

- Attach a small wrought iron rod over the window above the kitchen sink. Using vintage day-of-the-week tea towels, hang them from the rod, slightly overlapping them so you can still see each embroidered image.
- In a dressing room, start with a 36-in.-square scarf and fold it diagonally. After tying knots (with small tails) on each side, use wide satin or grosgrain ribbon to attach the scarf to a decorative rod.

Blinds and Shades

BLINDS AND SHADES HAVE PRACTICALITY AT THEIR CORE, controlling both light and privacy. But they're available in a vast assortment of designs, too. Horizontal blinds run the gamut from vinyl mini-blinds, often used in a kitchen and easy to clean, to Venetian blinds; replicating the original design that dates back to the 1840s, they offer a hint of nostalgia. Wooden blinds are another popular option; their ladder tapes, applied vertically on both sides of the blind, come in a wide variety of patterns and colors. Vertical blinds, meanwhile, are more contemporary in nature. Their slats can be encased in sheer fabric, allowing light to gently filter into a room.

Shades offer even more choices. There's everything from energy-saving honeycomb shades often found in a kitchen or bath to balloon shades, roller shades, even woven shades made of natural materials; they can all be just as plain or fancy as your decor dictates.

▲ A WHIMSICAL PRINT first appears on the window seat, then jumps right up to the Roman shade above. Navy blue ribbon trim echoes the room's predominant hue while emphasizing the width and length of the window.

◀ IN A ROOM FULL OF DISTINCT EDGES, soft balloon shades take the edge off. A single shade across this large window would have been difficult to raise and lower; this row of side-by-side shades is easier to handle and provides better control of lighting levels.

▲ DIFFERENT WINDOWS WITHIN THE SAME ROOM often call for diverse window treatments. They can co-exist peacefully, though, if they're made of the same fabric, proven in this living room by the draperies on one wall and Roman shades on either side of the fireplace.

Blinds vs. Shades

THE DIFFERENCE BETWEEN BLINDS AND SHADES is quite simple: Blinds have moving parts, whereas shades do not. The former includes horizontal and vertical blinds typically made of wood, vinyl, or metal. They can be closed for complete privacy or opened to allow light into a room. The latter category encompasses Roman shades, balloon shades, roller shades, and woven shades made of natural materials like bamboo. As a whole, shades provide more color and pattern options than blinds. Window shadings offer a cross between a blind and a shade; opaque fabric slats between two layers of sheer fabric can be tilted to control light and privacy.

▲ ROMAN SHADES IN A TROPICAL PRINT stand out against a more subdued wall covering in this West Indies–inspired bedroom. Rather than visually compete with the shades, simple matchstick blinds complement the warm wood tones of the room as well as the wicker chair.

◄ BALLOON SHADES can run the gamut from formal to completely casual, often depending on the way the shades are hung. In this kitchen, they're simply gathered on a rod, giving them the kind of informality that this room calls for.

Creative Pull Cords

PULL CORDS ARE A NECESSARY PART of some window treatments, but that doesn't mean you can't modify them. To turn a simple cord into one that's eye-catching, lower your blind or shade completely and measure the exact length of the remaining cord from top to bottom. Cut three pieces of ribbon that length, and then tie them securely at the top. Braid the ribbons tightly, incorporating the original cord with one of the lengths. Once you get to the bottom, add wooden, ceramic or glass beads, and then knot off the braid beneath them.

▶ SOFT, NEUTRAL HUES dominate this bedroom. To keep the quiet setting from becoming boring, however, a floral print was added to the mix in small doses—in the balloon shades, upholstered headboard, and pillow shams.

▼ ONE OF THE EASIEST WAYS to tie a decorating scheme together is to find one fabric and stick with it. That's the case here, where a floral stripe on a balloon shade reappears at the window seat, an armchair, and an ottoman.

Room-Darkening Strategies

CERTAIN CIRCUMSTANCES DICTATE that a room be completely dark—family and friends gathered in a media room to watch a movie, adults who work the night shift catching up on some sleep, and, of course, babies and toddlers taking afternoon naps. There are several ways to block light with window treatments. Draperies, curtains, and most shades can be given blackout linings. Even shades made of natural materials such as woven grasses can be backed with light-blocking fabrics. To ensure a complete light-blocking effect, opt for a layered look of treatments: Team up a light-blocking shade with heavyweight curtains or draperies that can be closed tightly.

▼ WHEN DEALING WITH MULTIPLE WINDOWS it's best to take a simple approach, especially when they curve like they do in this family room. Here, bamboo shades add just a touch of color. By keeping them raised or lowered to the same height, they act as a single unit.

ON EITHER SIDE OF THE FIRE-PLACE in this living room, tailored Roman shades echo the horizontal lines of the mantel between them. Meanwhile, on the adjacent wall, curtains made of the same cream-colored fabric provide privacy but pull back for easy access to the French doors.

ALTHOUGH THIS WINDOW TOPPER has the appearance of traditional balloon shades, it has a distinct difference. In fact, this is a balloon-style valance; it's stationary so that the owners can easily pass through the sliding glass doors.

IN THIS BEDROOM, three individual Roman shades on the long wall and a matching one just around the corner raise high enough to be able to appreciate the view beyond. Even when they're completely closed, though, you can see the sun or night sky through the arched window above.

▲ A STUNNING OUTDOOR VIEW dictates minimal window treatments. In this casual living area, white match-stick blinds provide all the light control and privacy that this room needs. The blinds pull up neatly to the tops of the windows, so they don't interfere with the verdant view.

◄ THE BLINDS IN THIS BATHROOM, readily available for any size window, offer the best of both worlds. Even when they're fully lowered, the louvers between the two layers of sheer fabric can be completely opened, allowing light to softly filter in.

▼ THIS WINDOW TREATMENT conveys a casual ambiance in keeping with the dining area's bistro feeling. A swagged Roman shade repeats the plaid of the chair cushions; matching flat panels dress the side windows, pulling back to reveal a solid yellow lining that echoes the color of the table and chairs.

▼ RATHER THAN MATCHING PRINTS, this homeowner opted to use complementary fabrics for a window seat and its companion window covering. While the seat cushion is covered in a small-scale plaid, the window—the larger element of the two—is dressed in two-tone stripe that's also grander in scale.

Shutters

SHUTTERS ARE APPRECIATED JUST AS MUCH FOR THEIR AESTHETIC VALUE as their practicality. Attached to the window frame, they become part of a room's architecture, their louvers creating a repeating horizontal pattern. When open, they allow sunshine to stream into a space; when closed, they're one of the most energy-efficient window treatments around. While they can provide a striking complement for soft curtains or draperies, they're also a stunning solution on their own, adding architectural interest to even the plainest room.

Most common are the traditional shutters and their Plantation-style counterparts. The former, characterized by 1¼-in. louvers, are well suited to small windows. Their narrow louvers brilliantly block the sun's rays. At the same time, however, they limit your view. Plantation shutters, better suited for large expanses of glass, commonly feature louvers that are between 2½ in. and 3½ in. wide. As a result, their large scale provides more drama—and a better view.

▶ WIDE OPEN, the shutters on these bathroom windows provide a memorable view. When closed, the louvers can be shut partially or completely—depending on the amount of privacy needed—and still allow plenty of natural light into the room.

▼ PLANTATION SHUTTERS can be fitted to windows and doors alike, providing any room with a completely cohesive backdrop. In this living room, it's all but impossible to tell the difference between the windows and doors.

▲ SIMPLE WHITE SHUTTERS become striking when set against a contrasting wall like this denim blue example. As if that weren't enough of an attention-getter, a shade in a spicy red plaid intensifies the drama.

▲ KEEPING A ROOM'S BACKDROP simple allows the furnishings to shine. That's the case in this living room, where neutral walls are interrupted only by windows dressed in plantation shutters in a similar shade. When the louvers are completely closed it almost seems like one continuous surround.

Measuring Up

BEFORE ORDERING ANY WINDOW TREATMENT, it's imperative that you have the right measurements. Use a steel measuring tape and always round up to the nearest ⅛ in. Treatments mounted inside the window frame require length and width measurements. For the length, measure from the bottom of the window frame to the top of the sill (*A*). For the width, measure from side to side within the frame (*B*). Measure at the top, the middle, and the bottom of the window; because your measurements may vary slightly, use the smallest number.

For treatments on the frame itself or on the wall, you'll also need to measure the area to the left (*C*) and to the right (*D*) of the window frame that will be covered. For shades, this may be only to the outside edge of the window frame; for draperies and curtains, it will depend on how wide you want the finished treatment to be. You'll also need to measure the distance from the top of the window opening up to the point where the hardware will be located (*E*). Finally, measure from the top of the sill down to the point at which you want your window treatment to stop (*F*).

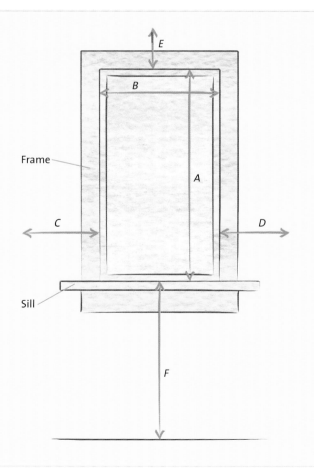

Wall Coverings

L ook around. The walls in your home measure up to have more square footage than any other surface. So why settle for hospital white? A vast variety of wall coverings exist today. Wallpaper is a traditional choice, but it includes a host of patterns appropriate for every style. Likewise, paint options have moved beyond a single color brushed on all four walls; bold color combinations and fancy decorative finishes are becoming the norm. In fact, you can choose almost anything that can be applied to a wall—fine fabric, wood paneling, reflective mirrors, and even gold leaf.

Before deciding on a wall covering, though, there are a few factors to keep in mind. If a room's furnishings are bold in terms of color and pattern, you'll want to keep the walls quiet and vice versa so one doesn't visually compete with the other. In addition, care and upkeep come into play, especially if children are part of your family; fingerprints and scuffmarks can be removed much more easily from scrubbable wallpapers and paints. But most important, make your walls an integral part of the decorating process instead of treating them as an afterthought. You'll be able to tell the difference in the end.

◄ THE CHECKERBOARD WALLS IN THIS DINING AREA were created with just two paint colors and a little masking tape. The oversize squares cause the eye to take giant steps from one square to the next, making the space appear bigger.

Paint

THE BEST ATTRIBUTES OF PAINT are that it's inexpensive and it offers instant gratification. Within hours of picking up a brush you can completely transform the look of a room. Even if you decide to use a single wall color, there are thousands of tints and shades to choose from. If you don't find the exact one you're looking for, ask your paint dealer to create a custom blend; he or she can precisely match a fabric, a flower, even a favorite shoe. On the other hand, if you're looking for something unique, consider the vast number of decorative finishes, from sponging and combing to marbling and leather looks.

Keep in mind, though, that with paint—as with most other things—you get what you pay for. A high-quality paint will typically last twice as long as its less-expensive counterpart, especially if it's applied with the right primer, which will make the paint go on smoother and provide better coverage, too.

◄ PAINT IS AN INEXPENSIVE SOLUTION to cabinet door replacement, providing an instant—and often unique—solution. The paint colors on these cabinets were inspired by the free-spirited tiles used on the backsplash.

How Much Paint Do You Need?

BUYING THE RIGHT AMOUNT OF PAINTS requires that you do some homework. Measure the perimeter of your room and multiply the total by the wall height. This will give you the square footage of your room's walls. (Don't deduct for windows, doors, or other openings unless they add up to more than 100 sq. ft.) If you want to paint the ceiling, too, multiply the width times the length to get the number of square feet. Divide the result by the number of square feet that a gallon of paint will cover. Round up to the nearest gallon, and then double it to accommodate two coats of paint.

▼ SIMPLICITY IS SOMETIMES THE BEST SOLUTION, as shown in this master bath, where a single paint color makes a dramatic statement. In a room full of bright white surfaces—from the tub all the way up to the ceiling—a cool purple hue on the walls provides a soothing surround.

▲ WIDE HORIZONTAL STRIPES ON THE WALLS of this entry make a stairwell almost disappear. Turning stripes on their side is typically a contemporary tactic, but it works equally well with an eclectic assortment of furnishings.

Make a Difference with Moldings

DECORATIVE MOLDINGS ADD INTEREST in otherwise plain and boxy rooms. One of the simplest additions is to add a chair rail around the room, 3 ft. to 4 ft. up from the floor or about a one-third of the way up the wall. The area below the chair rail can be painted, wallpapered, even paneled. The portion of the wall above the rail can be treated in a complementary fashion.

More impressive still can be crown moldings, a type of trim used to create visual interest where the walls meet the ceiling. These moldings can be purchased in pre-formed pieces at your local home center in wood or polyurethane, the latter of which has the look of plaster. They can be painted to match the rest of the room's woodwork, the same color as the walls or ceiling, or in a contrasting hue.

Last but not least, a decorative baseboard can also be added to a room. More often than not, it's best to paint or stain the baseboard to match the rest of the room's trim. You may be surprised, though, at the impact this kind of simple decorative embellishment can make.

BASEBOARD   CHAIR RAIL   CROWN MOLDING

▶ RED-GLAZED WALLS IN THIS LIVING ROOM create an instant sense of warmth and welcome. The rich hue not only coats the walls but also the crown molding at the ceiling level as well as the baseboard below, creating a spectacular, seamless effect.

◄ PAINT CAN CREATE THE ILLUSION OF FURNITURE, proven by this blue painted-on "canopy." Its curves are a welcome departure from the straight-forward design of the sleeping spot. In addition, it provides a strong dose of color, much needed in this otherwise subdued space.

TRICKS OF THE TRADE

Changing Spaces

ALTERING THE DIMENSIONS OF A ROOM doesn't require a major remodeling. Instead, you can achieve a similar effect with paint. If you have a long, tunnel-like room, for instance, consider painting the two long walls a lighter color such as cream and the two short ones a darker coffee hue. Because dark colors visually "advance"—seeming closer than they actually are—you'll create the effect of squaring up the space. Just varying the colors by two or three shades will make a dramatic difference.

You can take the same approach with ceilings, too. By painting the walls a light color and the ceiling a darker hue, you will seemingly lower the ceiling—a real plus in some older homes with soaring spaces. This trick works especially well in rooms where you want a cozy atmosphere. (It's not as successful in rooms with vaulted ceilings since these architectural assets are meant to create an open, airy feeling.) To take the concept one step further, bring the color of the ceiling down 6 in. to 8 in. onto the walls, and then add molding at the stopping point. This works especially well in kids' rooms as it brings things closer to their level.

▲ PAINTING THE CEILING slightly darker than the walls visually lowers it, giving the room a more intimate ambiance in the process. The yellow ceiling in this bathroom creates that cozy feeling and echoes the color of the counter and tub surround, tying the overall scheme together.

DECORATIVE FINISHES

▲ THE WALLS OF THIS LIVING
ROOM get extra dimension
thanks to a decorative paint
technique known as ragging,
achieved by applying two different
paint colors with a rag. Its three-
dimensional look is especially
effective in a room with low-key
colors because it creates visual
interest.

About Decorative Paint Finishes

COMBING IS ONE OF THE EASIEST DECORATIVE PAINT FINISHES to achieve. Just apply a base coat of paint; once dry, cover it with a glaze in a complementary color. While the glaze is still wet, pull the teeth of a combing tool through it, creating a striped effect. Other techniques include sponging and ragging. Using special sponges (found at a crafts store) or a bunched-up rag, lightly dab a complementary hue onto the wall, allowing some of the wall's dry base coat to show through.

Color blocking and marbling are other options. Because they're more complex, you may want to consult a paint professional for help.

Trompe l'Oeil

STRICTLY TRANSLATED, the French term trompe l'oeil means to "fool the eye." And it's done just that for centuries. The intent is to trick the viewer into thinking that a painted-on image is the real thing. It may be something as simple as clouds painted on a ceiling or an architectural element such as a niche incorporated into a room. If the technique is done well, you not only have to look—but also touch—the elements in question to determine whether they're imaginary or not.

This French technique, however, is not something that a novice painter should attempt. It takes a professional, one with extensive experience in creating believable three-dimensional effects. As an alternative, you may want to consider wallpaper that provides a similar appearance. It can be more cost effective and, more often than not, give you quicker results, as well.

▲ IN A ROOM DEVOID OF ARCHITEC-TURE, a little trompe l'oeil may be all that's needed to add visual interest. In this entry hall, the technique's three-dimensional character is evident in the painted-on niche, complete with a blue and white urn within.

▲ WHAT COULD HAVE BEEN AN ENTRY FULL OF LOOK-ALIKE DOORS gets a new dimension with trompe l'oeil bookshelves, complete with assorted volumes and accessories. The painted-on moldings and trim, in fact, are hard to distinguish from the real trim that surrounds the actual door.

◄ SOME CHANDELIERS ARE SUSPENDED from medallions, formal decorations often made of plaster, to give them more importance. This one gets the same effect with a painterly translation; a floral border rings the light fixture, making it seem larger in the process.

Brushing Up

THE RIGHT BRUSH can make a world of difference in any painting project. Basically, brushes can be categorized into those with natural bristles and those with synthetic. If you're using oil-based paints either one will do but for latex paints use only synthetic. Natural brushes absorb water from latex paints, which eventually makes them lose their shape. Likewise, there are specific brushes designated for specific tasks. Wall brushes that are 4 in. wide are appropriate for large flat surfaces while 3-in.-wide trim brushes are well suited for doors. Angled sash brushes, typically 1½-in. wide, are great for detail work.

▼ THE WHIMSICAL WALLS IN THIS BEDROOM were created by first painting on a pale lavender hue. The various patterns were then applied in a freehand fashion with white paint, right down to the vase of flowers that tops a "table" at the head of the bed.

▲ A COMBING TECHNIQUE CREATED the gingham-like pattern on these walls. First, a blue hue was applied. Once dry, it was painted over with a beige color; then the excess paint was wiped away using a comb, a tool with extra-wide teeth designed for this method.

Stencils and Stamping

STENCILED WALLS DATE BACK TO COLONIAL TIMES, so they are often associated with traditional interiors. Today, however, they have a place in all types of homes—from the most refined traditional to unmistakably modern. To create a stenciled wall, use a single pattern, purchased from a crafts store, or design one of your own that's more complex. By using multiple patterns you can even replicate the look of the most intricate wallpaper. Best of all, stenciling is inexpensive, easy to do, and requires little more than brushes, paint, and the pattern of your choice. Acrylic paints are most often used, preferred for their quick drying time, but interior latex paint is another option.

If you're looking for a similar effect with even less effort, consider stamping. All you need are rubber or foam stamps of the motifs that you want to use—found at any craft or art supply store—and some paint. Be sure to practice on the same kind of surface that you'll ultimately be working on before applying your pattern to the wall, so you'll know just how much pressure to apply.

▲ STENCILING BECAME POPULAR IN COLONIAL TIMES, before wallpaper was widely available. In this room, borders at the ceiling level and above the chair rail are separated with alternating leafy motifs. Stencils are available at any crafts store, but you can also make your own custom designs.

▲ TAKING A CUE FROM THE STARFISH that support these gauzy window treatments, seashell motifs are stamped directly on the walls, conveying a subtle ocean theme. Their pale colors keep them quietly in the background; anything darker would have created a jarring "dotted" effect.

Wallpaper

T HERE'S A REASON THAT WALLPAPER is a perennially popular wall covering. There's a style and price range to suit everyone. Plus, it's typically easy to install yourself. As long as you keep a few guidelines in mind, you really can't go wrong. If you have smooth-as-glass walls, almost any wallpaper will work. If you're trying to disguise cracking and peeling walls, though, you might opt for a heavy paper or use a liner with a lighter one. If it has a texture or pattern, that, too, will detract from any imperfections on the wall beneath.

When purchasing wallpaper keep in mind that the pattern and run numbers are printed on each roll; different dye lots do vary slightly, so make sure that all of your rolls are from the same run and that you buy a sufficient amount the first time. You can always return an extra roll—or find other creative ways to use it.

▲ A BLACK AND WHITE TOILE WALLPAPER adorns separate panels in this entry, the white woodwork between each pair emphasizing the pattern that much more. The black and white theme continues throughout the room, but in more simplified geometric forms to keep the attention squarely on the toile.

▼ A GOLD DAMASK PATTERN on the walls of this bedroom immediately establishes a rich ambiance. Damask is often used in more formal settings; here, that formality is carried out with a matching armchair, not to mention an elaborate silk window treatment and crystal chandelier.

▲ A SAILBOAT-PATTERNED WALLPAPER provides the starting point for this scheme. The reds and golds of the ships' hulls reappear in striped curtain panels as well as the trim on the valance and tray ceiling. The latter two elements are the same white as the sails, providing important visual relief.

▲ A RED AND WHITE FLORAL WALLPAPER was the inspiration for this bedroom's color scheme. Primarily white furnishings were chosen so they wouldn't compete with the complex pattern; the bed, the chair, and the small chest seem crisper against it while providing some much-needed visual relief.

Scale

WHETHER YOU REALIZE IT OR NOT, you probably have an innate sense of scale. You know instantly that a delicate spindle-back chair looks all wrong next to an oversize recliner. Likewise, a diminutive bedside table appears out of place next to a grand king-size bed. Simply put, scale refers to the relationship among furnishings within a room. But it's more than size that comes into play; visual weight is important, too.

Many people, for instance, flank a sofa with two end tables. If you don't want a matched set (and, in this age of eclecticism, that's the case more often than not), be sure that your selections are compatible in scale—with each other as well as with the sofa between them. For one end of a plush sofa, for instance, you may choose a set of nesting tables 2 in. taller than the sofa's arm; on the other end, you may opt for a small chest that's 2 in. lower. They both work with the height of the sofa and from a visual point of view, too. The multiple legs of the nesting tables balance the solid mass of the chest at the opposite end.

▲ INSPIRED BY A DECORATIVE SECRETARY FULL OF BOOKS, these owners took the library look a step further, surrounding the space with a trompe l'oeil wallpaper that has volumes stacked from floor to ceiling. Shared red and yellow hues tie the paper and furniture piece together.

▲ THE LARGE SCALE OF THIS PAISLEY WALLPAPER PATTERN is perfectly suited to the spacious entry that it's in. Because there is minimal furniture here, it's easier to appreciate the pattern, too.

◄ WALLPAPER IN A BOTANICAL PRINT takes center stage in this bedroom, thanks to its large-scale pattern. The paper's floral motifs are echoed in the canopy and the nearby table skirt. Meanwhile, the canopy's side curtains repeat the plaid of the companion valance but—without the floral aspect—offer subtle visual relief.

▼ TOSSING ASIDE THE OLD DECORAT-ING DICTUM that dark colors shouldn't be used in small spaces, this bathroom gets its cozy appeal from the dark blue hue. For continuity's sake, the sink repeats the blue and even the built-in shelves are wrapped with the dramatic wall covering.

◄ A PERFECTLY PENNED CURSIVE SCRIPT EMBELLISHES the wallpaper in this entrance hall. The black and white print provides a dramatic backdrop for the bright red Dutch door. Other fur-nishings are intentionally subdued, except for the curtains that repeat the pattern as well as its reverse.

BORDERS

▼ A BORDER AT THE CEILING LEVEL EMPHASIZES THE HEIGHT OF THIS ROOM, making it even seem taller in the process. Coordinating floral fabrics—in the same blue and white hues—appear on the curtains as well as the bed skirt and shams, bringing a strong sense of design continuity to the room.

▲ SOMETIMES ALL IT TAKES is a small amount of pattern to make a dramatic difference. Here, a fruit-laden border appears in the living room and then reappears in the kitchen beyond. The minimal accent goes a long way in tying together the two distinct spaces.

◄ BORDERS AREN'T LIMITED TO WALLPAPER. This lacey example, like so many triangular doilies marching across the wall, was painted right onto the faux-finished walls. At the same time, it softens the sharp angles of the room and seemingly lowers the height to baby's level.

TRICKS OF THE TRADE

Innovative Ways with Wallpaper

WITH JUST A LITTLE INGENUITY, you can come up with any number of ways to use wallpaper. Storage boxes, for instance, hold everything from a child's first drawings to family photos, but usually end up buried in the attic. Covering boxes of stepped-up sizes in a single wallpaper pattern—or choosing two or three that complement one another—can add to your decor. Set a stack of three next to an armchair to keep the treasures they hold close at hand and to provide nearby "tabletop" space.

Other possibilities include lining the back of a bookcase and covering a lampshade.

Tile

Think of tile and your mind goes immediately to the kitchen and bath. It's in these spaces, after all, where this wall covering is most efficient. It can stand up to high moisture and is easy to clean. Don't think, though, that all this practicality means that you have to give up anything in terms of style. In fact, tiles present some of today's most stylish design solutions, whether they're highly decorative, forming an elaborate mural, or solid in color but installed in a creative way.

Ceramic tiles, with myriad colors and almost as many patterns and textures, are still predominant, but there are other options. Shimmering glass mosaics, for instance, can add sparkle to a space. When laying out your tile pattern don't assume that white grout is your only option, either. It can be tinted to subtly blend into the overall design. Or use a contrasting color for an entirely different look.

▲ FRUIT-LADEN TILES, APPLIED IN A FREEFORM FASHION, add plenty of color and pattern to the kitchen, a room often filled with solid, linear surfaces. So that a pattern with this much panache doesn't overwhelm, keep other elements in the room subdued and the bold tiles to a minimum.

▼ WHITE TILES ARE A GOOD WAY TO MAKE A BATHROOM LOOK ESPECIALLY CLEAN. So that it doesn't look too sanitized, however, it's important to incorporate some color, even a minimal amount. Here, peach-colored trim adds a splash of warm color in an otherwise all-white room.

▼ WITH SO MANY NECESSARY ELEMENTS, it can be a challenge to create a bath that's visually sound. This one solves the potential problem with color; ceramic wall tiles in the same slate blue as the vanity and the tub surround create consistency—and a subdued atmosphere.

▲ MOSAIC TILES IN SHADES OF GOLD line the wall behind the sink in this bathroom. The glass vanity allows you to better appreciate the floor-to-ceiling ceramics. Nearby, a contemporary wall covering repeats the geometric shape of the mosaics while providing an eye-catching contrast in scale.

▲ OCEAN BLUE TILES surround the entire space in this contemporary bath. Around the shower, rippled glass provides the necessary enclosure—and mimics ocean waves—providing a contrast in texture and still allowing the blue hue of the tile to show through.

▼ STANDARD, AFFORDABLE TILES can add punch to any room. Sometimes all it takes is a creative application. Here, a simple four-square configuration of blue and white tiles makes a strong, successful statement.

▲ TO STRETCH YOUR DECORATING DOLLAR, choose a single wall to make a dramatic impact. This kitchen bump-out features colorful mosaic tiles on the far wall, interrupted only by a glass-block window that repeats the square geometry in a larger scale.

▲ PLAIN WHITE TILES can be less expensive than their colored, more decorative counterparts. To cut costs without sacrificing style, this bath uses white mosaic tiles in the tub surround and behind the sink, with interspersed blue and green tiles providing just enough color to create a subtle design.

Decorating Ideas: Glass Block

MORE OFTEN THAN NOT, glass block is thought of as a building material. It's typically used for divider walls, where you want some semblance of privacy in one or both areas but still need light to pass through. Similarly, you'll find it used in lieu of conventional windows, particularly in a bathroom. Today, however, it has crossed over into the decorative realm. Available in square or rectangular shapes—and in various colors, too—glass block can have all kinds of applications. In a contemporary room, a row of glass block over a window might form a kind of light-filtering "cornice." Along the back of a kitchen island it might provide an interesting ledge.

When shopping for glass block, most often available through window suppliers, you'll find a wide range of textures, too, from those that are completely smooth to those that have a frosted finish or a ribbed surface. There's even an alternative to heavyweight glass; if you don't want all the weight of real glass blocks consider acrylic look alikes.

▲ GLASS BLOCKS ARE USED IN AN INNOVATIVE WAY IN THIS MASTER BATH; standing on end, they define the the bathing area. Because they're backlit, the gently curved spa and tub area is emphasized. Along the back wall, tiles with a similar glassy sheen add more translucence to the room.

Fabric

WHETHER YOU WANT TO MAKE A FASHION STATEMENT or cover up a less-than-perfect wall, fabric is often the best answer. Unlike wallpaper, it can be applied in a variety of ways. You can glue it, nail it, or staple it right onto the wall; add a layer of batting beneath it and you have a great sound and heat insulator. Or, you can pleat it, gather it, or even drape it.

Fabric can even be used to create a wall where there isn't one. Take a cue from the Victorian era and curtain off a doorway, for instance; when privacy is a priority, simply pull the curtains shut. Likewise, you might suspend a floor-length curtain from a rod affixed to the ceiling, using it to partition a room.

▲ FABRIC "WALLS" ARE PRACTICAL, good-looking, and flexible. The blue and white curtains surrounding this dining area are left open during the day, framing the doorways from which they're hung. For evening entertaining, though, they're closed to create a more intimate atmosphere.

◄ A MULTICOLOR STRIPE not only lines these walls but also dresses the windows, making them all but disappear when the curtains are closed. A black-painted baseboard and ceiling-level trim provide stopping points for the pattern. Similarly, dark neutral hues frame a portrait and the twin beds.

► IN A ROOM DEVOTED to a single color, a variety of textures is necessary for visual interest. The blue hue here is sleek and smooth on the upholstered bed with a quilted cover providing a welcome contrast. Behind the bed, a wall of gathered fabric adds more texture.

▼ A RED-AND-WHITE TOILE FABRIC LITERALLY COVERS THIS SPACE. To provide visual balance, pattern is kept to a minimum elsewhere in the room; a red and white striped sofa gives an almost-contemporary counterpoint, while other elements, right down to the rug, are all in solid colors.

Screen Stars

HISTORICALLY, DECORATIVE SCREENS were used to provide privacy in the bedroom. Placed in one corner, they served as small dressing areas. While that function is still perfectly feasible, today's screens have moved beyond the bedroom, taking on a wide variety of roles. A screen, for instance, might divide an area into two smaller spaces, separating a television-viewing area at one end of the room from a cozy reading corner at the other. Likewise, a screen can have a purely practical purpose. It can discreetly hide a storage area; in a home office, you can stack boxes of files several feet high.

Screens can be purely decorative, too. On a fabric-covered screen, you might even use two different materials to give each side a distinct look—a solid color on one side and a pattern on the other. Some of today's styles can even add architectural dimension to a room, showcasing fine woods and intricately carved details. You'll find, too, that a few of the most contemporary styles are nothing more than a metal framework, becoming almost sculptural in their appearance.

▲ DECORATIVE SCREENS PROVIDE VISUAL INTEREST and extra dimension against otherwise ordinary walls. Here, a scrolling pattern creates a much more interesting backdrop for the pedestal table which, otherwise, may have gotten lost in the room.

The Fifth Wall

WHEN DRESSING THE WALLS OF YOUR ROOM, keep in mind that there are typically five, not four. Just look up. The ceiling, or fifth wall, deserves just as much attention as its counterparts. Plus, it provides an accent opportunity, be it subtle or bold. Something as simple as painting the ceiling a shade or two darker than the walls can create a more intimate ambiance. Or take a more daring approach and paint the ceiling a contrasting color. For instance, in a room with a blue and green floral wallpaper, pull out the bright yellow hue that appears only in the flowers' centers and splash it across the ceiling.

Similarly, use a wallpaper on the ceiling that complements the one used throughout the rest of the room. In short, any application that's appropriate for conventional walls can be used on the ceiling, too.

▼ NIGHT SKIES ON THE CEILING ARE APPROPRIATE IN A NURSERY, where babies are forever napping. Here, the walls work their way up to darker and darker hues of blue, leading to a star-scattered sky. Lighting tucked behind the molding illuminates the edges of night the sky.

◄ IN THIS MASTER BATH, a ceiling inset is hand-painted with bamboo latticework that's interspersed with leaves. Reminiscent of the view just beyond the French doors, it takes the viewer's eye straight up, making the already tall room seem to soar even higher in the process.

► IN LIEU OF THE TRADITIONAL plaster medallion surrounding a chandelier, this ceiling has the face of a clock encircling the area. The clock's dark color replicates that of the floor below, linking the two surfaces and creating a more intimate dining space.

▼ CLOUDS ARE OFTEN A POPULAR choice for a trompe l'oeil ceiling. They seem even more believable, though, in a room that has a dome ceiling. Here, eyebrow windows enable the sun's rays to brighten the scene.

Floor Coverings

After walls, floors are the largest area where you can add dramatic impact. At the same time, however, they have to be practical. Because there is something stylish for every budget, start by figuring how much you have to spend. Next, consider the space itself; who will be using it and how? Do you have a young family that dictates easy-to-clean vinyl tile in the kitchen? Or do you have pets that would see a sisal rug as their personal scratching pad?

A vast assortment of floor coverings is available. Carpet includes wall-to-wall options as well as area rugs and natural fibers such as seagrass and bamboo. Hardwood has its own variations, too, ranging from light to dark and from narrow to very wide. Resilient flooring encompasses vinyl as well as rubber and cork. Meanwhile, nonresilients include everything from ceramic tile to stone. But flooring decisions become even more complicated because some types replicate others. For instance, vinyl can mimic the look of marble, giving you the function of the former and the look of the latter—all without spending a fortune. The bottom line: You can have anything you set your sights on.

◄ THE HARDWOOD FLOOR in this living area quietly underscores the profusion of color throughout the rest of the room. It's layered with a burnt orange area rug that not only defines the main conversation area but also inspires the overall color scheme.

Carpet

THERE'S NOTHING LIKE THE FEELING OF CARPET under your bare feet. But its advantages are much more far-reaching than comfort. Color and pattern are high on its list of assets; the right carpet can be the starting point for a scheme or provide a stunning focal point. In addition, it reduces noise and conserves energy.

Carpet options include synthetics, such as nylon and polyester, and natural fibers, such as wool and silk. Whatever your preference, be sure that you purchase the best that your budget allows, especially for high-traffic areas. One quality test is to check the number of yarns per square inch; the higher the number, the better. Also be sure to perform the "grin" test. Fold a carpet sample back (forming the floor covering's "grin") and look to see how much of the backing is exposed. The less backing you see, the denser—and more long lasting—your carpet will be.

▼ A MULTICOLOR RUG is a success in this hallway, largely because the brilliant floor covering is set against a subtle backdrop. Fronting a sofa—the perfect place to sit down to change shoes and boots—it helps create the feeling of a room within a room.

▲ IN THIS MASTER RETREAT, wall-to-wall carpet provides a hint of pattern yet doesn't compete with the other furnishings in the room. Its two-tone neutral coloration blends beautifully with the color palette, while the diagonal pattern seemingly stretches the dimensions of the room.

Defining Carpet Types

WE OFTEN THINK OF COLOR AND PATTERN **when shopping for carpet. But equally important is the type and how it will stand up to daily use. Basically, carpet can be categorized into three types:**

- **Cut-pile:** The yarns are sheared at the top, allowing them to stand straight up. Referred to as "plush," it's used in bedrooms and living rooms.

- **Loop-pile:** The loops are left intact, making it durable and therefore ideal in high-traffic areas.
- **Cut-and-loop pile:** Combining cut-and-loop pile carpets, it takes on a subtle, sculpted pattern. It's a good option in heavily trafficked areas because footprints are disguised by the carpet pattern.

▲ IN THIS CHILD'S PLAYROOM, a navy blue carpet is edged at one end with a wave of yellow. Multicolored stars set into the field create the effect of a night sky, providing a contrast to the sunny skyscape painted on the storage wall.

► WHEN COMBINING MULTIPLE CARPETS, it's best to vary colors instead of styles. The red, yellow, and blue carpets that come together here are all the same plush type; thus, everything is on the same level and there's no danger of tripping.

Stairway Runners

A CARPET RUNNER GOING UP A SET OF STAIRS is a can't-miss way to keep consistency throughout the house. These narrow rugs and carpets act as decorative elements, leading the eye from one level of a home to another. But they have a practical purpose, too. Not only do they diminish the wear and tear on stair treads—and the accidental kicking of stair risers, for that matter—but they also keep noise to a minimum. A dark color can even disguise the tracks of children going up and down several times a day.

A carpet runner presents a multitude of design opportunities, too. It can quietly blend into the stair steps beneath it, creating one cohesive scheme. Or it can provide a stark contrast, taking on an almost sculptural quality in the process. It should create a sense of connection, mixing beautifully with decorative elements on the first floor and matching those on the second—or the upstairs hall, at the very least.

▲ STAIR RUNNERS PROVIDE A UNIQUE OPPORTUNITY to showcase a floor covering in a more three-dimensional way; at the same time, they muffle the sound of people going up and down. The diamond-patterned runner on this staircase is the perfect foil for another geometric shape—the green and white stripe on the walls.

◀ A BLACK AND WHITE SCHEME IN THIS ENTRY HALL gives every element more emphasis. The hardwood floor is painted a jet black, providing a stark contrast to the rest of the all-white architecture. Softening the look is a plush black runner that leads the eye from one painted floor to the next.

▲ BRAIDED RUGS, WITH THEIR STRONG COLONIAL ROOTS, are often thought of as being done in dark colors. This modern-day translation, though, weaves bright reds, whites, and blues into its design, inspiring upholstered chairs, slipcovers, and window toppers in the same vibrant shades.

▲ A SUBTLE COLOR DIFFERENCE between this sculpted area rug and the hardwood floor allows them to complement, rather than compete with, one another. The sculpted pattern is important. Without it, the rug would have been too plain for this formal setting.

Sizing Up Rugs

WHETHER PAGING THROUGH A CATALOG or shopping in a store, it's hard not to notice that most area rugs are available in standard sizes. They vary from those just large enough to put in front of the kitchen sink to those that will fill an entire room. More and more provide custom options, too, not only in terms of sizes but also in types of bindings. Dimensions will vary slightly but you'll generally find rugs in these sizes: 2 ft. by 3 ft., 3 ft. by 5 ft., 4 ft. by 6 ft., 5 ft. by 8 ft., 6 ft. by 9 ft., 8 ft. by 10 ft., and 9 ft. by 12 ft. Runners up to 12 ft. long are also readily available, as are round and square shapes.

▼ ORIENTAL RUGS ADD MUCH-NEEDED COLOR and pattern in this kitchen awash in neutral hues. At the same time, one defines a sitting spot near the French doors while the other directs traffic to adjacent rooms.

Liner Notes

SOMETIMES, IT'S WHAT LIES UNDER THE SURFACE that counts. Almost any carpet will last longer—and feel better underfoot—with the right lining (the specific type varies according to the carpet style).

Equally essential are liners for area rugs to keep them from slipping and sliding. There are two basic types. The first is used between a rug and a hard surface (a hardwood floor, for instance) to keep the area rug from slipping. The second is used between a rug and another soft surface (carpet, for example). In this case, the liner keeps the area rug from "creeping."

▶ AN ORIENTAL RUG AT THE FOOT of this four-poster visually defines a small sitting area. The colors blend with the carpet beneath it but there's enough pattern to make a distinction between the two.

Area Rug Types

BY DEFINITION, AN AREA RUG is a floor covering that only partially covers a floor. Here are characteristics of a few perennial favorites:

- **Aubusson:** This tightly woven wool tapestry-style rug is flat-woven, making it extremely durable.
- **Braided:** Typically round or oval in shape, this rug type is made of one continuous wool or cotton braid.
- **Oriental:** Authentic Oriental rugs are hand-knotted of wool or silk, making them one of the most expensive options. Oriental-design rugs (machine-made reproductions) offer less-expensive alternatives.
- **Kilim:** These casually elegant wool rugs are flat woven and characterized by small vertical slits in the floor covering where two colors meet.
- **Dhurrie:** Made of cotton or wool, a dhurrie rug is also flat woven and features tribal motifs similar to those found in a kilim.

▲ BEFITTING OF A CASUALLY ELEGANT DINING AREA, this needlepoint rug solidly anchors the table and chairs. It's large enough to serve as the room's focal point and, perhaps more important, allow diners enough room to push back their chairs without catching them on the rug's edge.

NATURAL FIBERS

▼ A SEAGRASS RUG, WITH A SUBTLE PATTERN woven right into it, has natural good looks befitting this room or any casual area. It's durable, too, although it can feel scratchy on bare feet.

▲ TO KEEP THINGS VISUALLY INTERESTING IN A NEUTRAL ROOM, a variety of texture is imperative. Here, a coarse sisal rug contrasts—in color and texture—with the smooth hardwood floor that it's set on. A hard slate-top table and soft upholstered chair lend additional texture.

◄ A SISAL FLOOR COVERING keeps things casually elegant in this living room. While a more formal carpet might have made it seem stilted, this natural option gives the setting approachable appeal.

What Size Area Rug?

To a large degree, choosing the size of an area rug comes down to personal preference. You may be looking for a rug to underscore a coffee table. Or you may be searching for something to put in the front entry. There are certain situations, though, that require you follow some guidelines. If you're shopping for a rug that will define a conversation grouping, start by putting your floor plan on paper. Then experiment with standard rug sizes. The right rug will accomplish one of two things: It will either be large enough so that all of your seating pieces will fit comfortably on top of it or it will be at least large enough for the front legs of each to fit. As a general rule, the sofa shouldn't be completely on the rug while an accompanying chair has only two legs on it. Likewise, in the dining room, an area rug beneath your table and chairs should be big enough so that, when a seated diner pushes back the chair, the back legs don't get caught in the process.

▲ AREA RUGS ARE ONE OF THE EASIEST WAYS to delineate spaces in a large room. Two area rugs, matched in color and style but not in size, visually divide this room into two distinct seating areas. Both rugs are large enough to comfortably accommodate their respective groupings.

Hardwoods

Hardwood flooring complements everything from traditional to contemporary settings. Even better, it's easy to care for and it can be refinished to restore its original beauty. Oak is the most popular species, thanks to its durability. But there is a wealth of other species available, too, including maple, cherry, even pecan. If you're looking for something more rustic, consider reclaimed lumber.

Because hardwood floors are easily damaged by water, they have to be sealed. Most of the flooring available at your local home center comes prefinished but if you're putting in a custom floor it will need to be finished once it's installed. You can go the more traditional route with penetrating oil followed up with wax or opt for simple waterproof polyurethane. Prefinished floors are good choices for rooms that use a single style throughout—a 3-in.-wide plank, for instance. Custom floors, however, allow more options such as incorporating a medallion or a decorative border.

▲ PLANK FLOORING is an especially smart choice for narrow spaces such as this hallway; its extrawide dimensions give the appearance of stretching the width of the passageway. Here, the antique-looking flooring provides a surprising—but appealing—contrast for the more contemporary wire stairwell.

◄ THIS DINING ROOM FLOOR, made of mesquite, has a rich grain that varies from light to dark, adding a decorative touch of its own. It provides an interesting contrast, from visual and textural points of view, to the slate floor in the adjacent kitchen.

▼ YELLOW WALLS, WHITE WOODWORK, AND A PALE HARDWOOD FLOOR create a light and airy ambience in this formal entry. While a darker floor would have matched the banister, it would have been too heavy for the large expanse of space, since the wood is also carried up the stairs.

▲ THE CHERRY WOOD IN THIS STORAGE WALL is used on the floor as well. Large squares of cherry are inlaid in front of the cabinetry, surrounded by darker borders for emphasis. The result: Each one encourages lingering at strategic spots, eventually leading to the next room.

▲ A HARDWOOD FLOOR in this eating area echoes the wood of the built-in banquette. The diagonal placement of the floorboards keeps the look lively; had they been placed at a right angle to the table and bench, the space would have seemed more reserved.

▲ NARROW-STRIP HARDWOOD FLOORING is a particularly good choice for a kitchen or any other area with constant traffic. Its narrow width means more support joints, standing up well to daily wear and tear.

Laminate Options

L AMINATES OFFER THE LOOK OF WOOD FLOORING, but can be far more practical. Most are made with a four-ply construction that consists of a backing, a moisture-resistant fiberboard, a decorative layer, and a tough "wear" layer on top that can have a high or low luster. The decorative layer looks amazingly real because it's actually a photograph of wood that's been sandwiched between layers.

The beauty of laminates—available in planks or tiles— lies in the fact that they can be installed on top of almost any kind of subfloor, including concrete and other wood. They're highly durable, too, more water and scratch resistant than their real-wood counterparts. That makes them particularly appropriate for kitchens and laundry rooms, and in homes that have children and pets. If your laminate floor should get damaged, it usually can't be repaired or refinished like wood. While some manufacturers offer putty with which to make repairs, you're better off replacing the damaged pieces of flooring.

▲ LAMINATE FLOORING OFFERS the rich look of hardwood with more durability and less care. Laminate options aren't limited to wood, either. Other choices include tile, slate, marble, and even granite.

PAINTED FLOORS

▼ AGAINST A PREDOMINANT PERIWINKLE BLUE, this room's bright white elements—the bathtub, beadboard walls, and decorative shelves—appear even more crisp and clean. The two tones affect each other in the same way on the floor, where a painted-on diamond pattern ties everything together.

THE LARGER THE PATTERN YOU PUT ON YOUR FLOOR, the more expansive the space appears. That works to perfection in this living room, where a large-scale diamond pattern seemingly increases its dimensions. Small, interspersed black diamonds, meanwhile, provide a smart but simple finishing touch.

TO MAKE A WOOD FLOOR KID FRIENDLY, consider painting a whimsical design such as this assortment of colorful game boards. A coat of polyurethane on top not only protects the motifs but also prevents children from getting splinters.

Painting Wood Floors

MAYBE YOU HAVE A LESS-THAN-PERFECT HARDWOOD FLOOR. Or you just want to express your creativity. Painted floors can be the solution to both situations, invariably giving you handsome results. Design options run the gamut from simple checkerboard patterns to stenciled images to elaborate trompe l'oeil effects. Before you go to all that effort, though, be sure that you use paint specially formulated for floor use. You can also use latex paint, as long as it's of a high quality. Just be sure, when finished, to protect your design with a coat of polyurethane.

Resilient Flooring

RESILIENT FLOORING TYPICALLY FINDS ITS WAY into everyone's home in one form or another. Characteristically softer and quieter than other flooring options, it ranges from vinyl to rubber to cork, even linoleum. Popular until the 1960s when easy-care vinyl was introduced (linoleum required almost weekly waxing), it is now making a comeback.

As a whole, resilient flooring is easy to maintain, making it a good choice for kitchens, bathrooms, laundry rooms, and mudrooms. Some types are available in sheet form—up to 12 ft. wide—but they come in 12-in. tiles, too, allowing you to be as creative as you'd like. Although it can be one of the least expensive flooring choices, its resiliency makes it susceptible to dents and gouges. If the dings are noticeable, you can patch sheet flooring or replace the affected tile and nobody will ever be the wiser.

▲ SPRING GREEN WALLS create a refreshing feeling in this children's bathroom, with the color splashed across the walls, then reappearing in vinyl flooring as an accent. The warm heart-pine countertop and naturally finished vanity provide just the right touch of warmth to the cool scheme.

◄ IT'S HARD TO BEAT the crisp and clean effect of a black-and-white checkerboard floor. The vinyl tiles are doubly dramatic as they repeat of the pattern of the dining table.

▲ IN THIS EATING AREA, a hand-cut linoleum floor creates the look of a "rug" under the table and chairs.
Red and gold tiles go only to the edge of the rug's border, but make you think they go right under it, too.

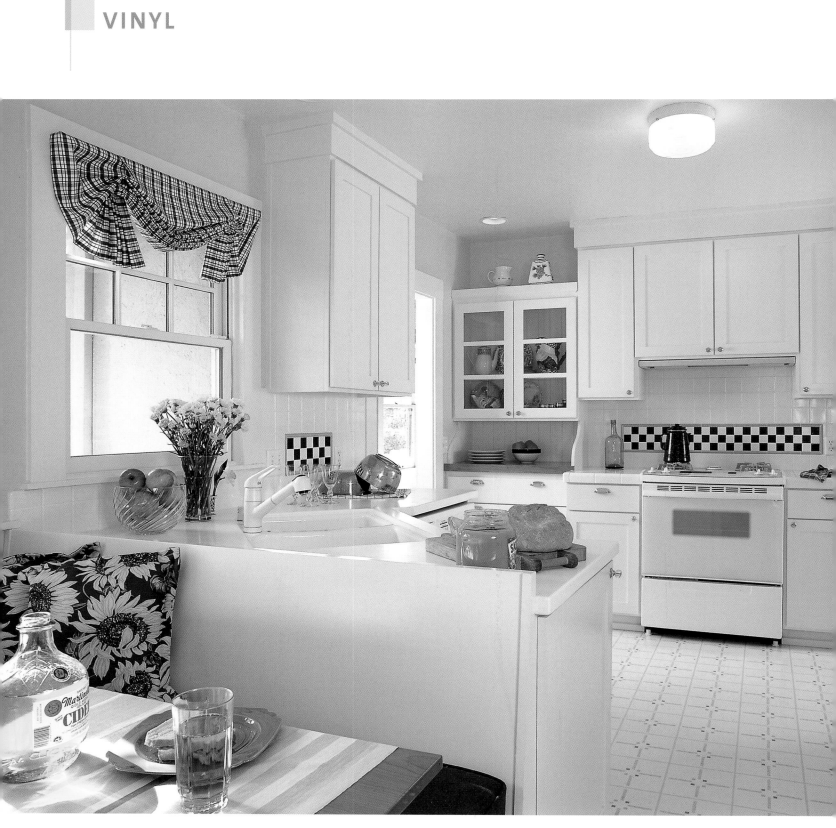

▲ IN A KITCHEN, WHERE THERE'S TYPICALLY SOLID-COLOR CABINETRY, it's important to create visual interest in some other way. Here, a geometric pattern is introduced in the form of squares, first in the vinyl flooring, again in the tiled backsplash, and finally, in the blue plaid window treatment.

Linoleum

LINOLEUM WAS ONCE THE FLOORING OF CHOICE in most kitchens. And, today, it's making a comeback, largely because it's durable and contains no synthetic chemicals like vinyl does. In the 1930s and 1940s, linoleum—its name derived from the main ingredient, linseed oil—was made in a wide variety of designs. Today's options are more limited; the most recent incarnation of linoleum features more neutral offerings either in 6-ft. rolls or in tile form. The latter option makes it easier to create custom floor designs with multiple colors. There is a drawback, however: Linoleum is not a do-it-yourself endeavor so professional installation is usually required.

▲ VINYL TILES PROVIDE a wealth of design opportunities, exemplified in this kitchen where a striped effect makes the space seem longer. The predominant silver grays of the flooring reflect the colors of aluminum furnishings and stainless-steel appliances, while the secondary browns bring in the color of the cabinetry.

▶ VINYL SHEET FLOORING comes in widths up to 12 ft., more often than not enough to make seams a thing of the past. That's an advantage when you have an intricate pattern that you don't want to interrupt, such as this stone-and-wood-strip combination.

CORK AND RUBBER

▶ BEYOND ITS SUBTLE TEXTURE AND NEUTRAL COLOR that goes with virtually any scheme, cork flooring has another advantage: Its gentle "give" provides one of the most resilient floor coverings, comfortable in rooms such as the kitchen where you find yourself on your feet.

Cork Designs with a Difference

I T MAY COME AS A SURPRISE that cork has been a viable flooring option for more than a century. It's always been known for its comfort and durability, but today's versions are sealed to make them moisture resistant, too. Another advantage is that they don't require waxing, like cork floors of the past.

You'll find cork available in planks or tiles. The latter gives you plenty of pattern options, particularly when you consider how many colors are available. The options go well beyond cork's natural beige to include scarlet red, royal blue, spring green—even lilac and burnt orange. All can be custom cut to the pattern of your choice, but standard patterns, such as simple grids and herringbones, are available, too.

▲ THE PATTERN POSSIBILITIES OF CORK FLOORING run the gamut from side-by-side, solid-color tiles to intricate, almost three-dimensional patterns like this one. Such design options rival some of the most beautiful parquet floors.

◀ RUBBER FLOORING MAKES PERFECT SENSE IN A BATHROOM; it's like one giant bathtub mat. Its nonslip surface isn't its only advantage, either; the raised-dot pattern provides visual interest in a room often inundated with stark white fixtures.

▼ IN A KITCHEN WITH ALL-WHITE CABINETRY the focal point has to come from somewhere else. In this case it's the ocean blue rubber floor. To further emphasize the color, it's repeated in the dining chairs and even the table base.

Nonresilient Flooring

I F YOU'RE NOT SURE WHAT "NONRESILIENT" FLOORING IS, just think in terms of hard surfaces. A wide variety of flooring fits into this category—ceramic and terra-cotta quarry tiles, marble, slate, brick, and concrete. Each one offers a striking look on its own (even concrete, with today's wide variety of paints and stains). And any one type can be paired with another flooring material—an inlay of hardwood, for instance, or a sisal rug simply thrown on top.

Most nonresilient flooring requires a sealer to make it impervious to spills and stains. With that finishing touch, it's appropriate for almost any application. There are drawbacks, though. The subfloor needs to be fairly level to keep joints, or the materials themselves, from cracking. Nonresilient flooring can be expensive, too, especially marble and slate, and its hard surface isn't very forgiving—whether you're standing on it for long periods of time or you happen to drop a dish.

▼ LARGE SLATE TILES, rich in varied neutral shades, are all the color that this room needs, with the exception of a sculptural-looking plant. The free-form leaves, in fact, provide a welcome contrast to the hard-edged slate, as does the nearby vanity with a curvaceous base.

▲ THESE SQUARE TILES MAY APPEAR TO BE ARTFULLY BROKEN to accommodate their leafy companions. In fact, the ground tiles and their artistic counterparts—perfectly suited for a solarium or garden room—arrive in perfect formation from the manufacturer; all you have to do is to add the grout.

▲ IT'S ESPECIALLY IMPORTANT IN AN ENTRYWAY that the flooring doesn't trip you up. The fieldstone used here solves that potential problem; it's been tumbled to smooth the surfaces and the edges.

CERAMIC TILE

▲ SOLID-COLOR TILES IN BLACK, WHITE, AND GRAY form an intricate plaid pattern in this garden room. The oversize design is a welcome change of pace in a space that is otherwise full of solid colors, from the built-in storage to the blue-painted door and the solid white walls.

About Tile

- **Glazed tile:** The most common type of ceramic tile, it is clay-based and available in a wide variety of shapes, patterns, and colors, some even replicating stone.
- **Porcelain tile:** This fine-grained and smooth ceramic tile has a certain elegance, it's available in matte, unglazed, or highly polished finishes.
- **Quarry tile:** Typically made of clay, and available glazed or unglazed, this more casual tile is usually dark red, although brown and gray can be found.

▲ ALTHOUGH THE FLOOR TILES IN THIS BATHROOM DON'T MATCH, they do mix—thanks to similar patterns and colors. With so much going on in the floor, it's important that the rest of the room be subdued. The only other pattern here appears in a window treatment, balancing the floor colors.

▶ NOT JUST ANY BLUE TILE FLOOR, this one exemplifies what you can do with variations on a color theme. The blue hues throughout range from light to dark and no less than half a dozen different tiles sizes have been incorporated into this work of art.

▲ CERAMIC TILES TEAM UP WITH HARDWOOD SPACERS IN THIS ENTRYWAY FLOOR, echoing the simple two-tone scheme established by the front door and the columns that flank it. The look steps right down into the living area, too, accomplished with hardwood treads and tile risers.

▶ MOSAIC TILES ARE ARTFULLY ARRANGED in this master bath, replicating the look of an Oriental rug in pastel tones. It's positioned where the real thing would be, too—squarely in front of the bathtub. Surrounding the "rug" are plain white tiles, intentionally keeping quiet in the background.

▼ LARGE TILES, LIKE THE 12-IN. EXAMPLES in this kitchen, make a floor seem more expansive than smaller ones would. Taking the design down to the last detail, the grout is tinted a gray-green which hides dirt better and complements the green hues in the room.

Tile Safety Tips

BEFORE INSTALLING CERAMIC TILE there are some practical matters to consider, the most important of which is safety. Particularly in a bathroom, where ceramic tile is a popular choice, be sure that your flooring isn't accident prone. Use tile that has a nonslip surface; you'll find ratings that specify them as such. Likewise, be careful about what you place on top of a tile floor. Rugs should have rubber backings and, in a child's bathroom, small step stools should have nonskid feet. Finally, minimize ways that water can find its way onto the floor, as it will only multiply the safety hazards.

BRICK, SLATE, AND QUARRY TILE

▲ ALTHOUGH QUARRY TILE COMES UNGLAZED AND REQUIRES SEALING IN WET AREAS, the resulting look is worth it, especially with hexagon-shaped tiles like these that make the floor a focal point. Its inherent clay color adds a welcome touch of warmth in a space that can sometimes seem sterile.

▲ THE SIMPLICITY OF SLATE IS PERFECTLY SUITED to understated Asian-style rooms. Here, a slate tile floor echoes the material found in the counter, allowing the *shoji*-style doors and wok-like sink to take center stage.

▲ BRICK FLOORING lends a casual ambience to this solarium and can stand up to the sun's warm rays. The warm red hues are a good balance, too, for the lush greenery inside and just beyond the windows.

Concrete Floors

CONCRETE FLOORS AREN'T JUST FOR BASEMENTS any-more. These days they're appearing through-out the house, particularly in contemporary interiors. Why? For starters, they're no longer limited to the drab gray that they once were. Both slab and poured concrete floors can be stained any number of designer colors. Likewise, the shade of your choice can be incorporated right with the cement when it is mixed. It goes without saying, too, that concrete's low cost is a distinct advantage—not to mention that it's extremely durable and easy to clean. It does, however, need to be sealed or it can stain. It's well worth the effort, though, as a sealed floor will develop a soft patina over time.

A lesser-known type of concrete flooring can also be found in tile form. It comes in a vast assortment of textures, some of them even replicating the look of marble and limestone.

▲ IN THIS MULTIPURPOSE ROOM, with laundry facilities and a double sink on one side and a shower on the other, an easy-to-clean concrete floor is perfectly suited to all tasks.

Storage Solutions

Storage is about more than closets. No matter how many closets you have, there aren't enough. For that matter, there's never sufficient storage space of any kind. But there are plenty of creative ways to incorporate storage. Sometimes, all it takes is a change of scene to give a piece of furniture a new lease on life. The armoire that houses the television set in the family room today might serve as off-season storage in the guest room tomorrow. Likewise, a chest that originally takes its place in the entry, providing drawer storage for scarves and mittens, can work equally well in a dining room, keeping table linens close at hand. Multipurpose pieces like these can move from one room to another as your family grows and your needs change.

Although some pieces, such as china cabinets, have specific uses, you'll find that most storage is flexible. If, for example, you find a bedside chest that could serve as a message center in the kitchen, put it where you need it most. The important thing is not to get tied down by furniture labels. It's one of the best ways to create personal style.

◀ CHINA CABINETS ARE OFTEN LARGE ENOUGH to hold a vast collection of dinnerware, making them the focal point of a room. Because this one is tucked into an architectural niche and its light wood tones blend quietly into the backdrop, it's eye catching without being overwhelming.

Chests

CHESTS ARE AVAILABLE IN EVERY IMAGINABLE STYLE. Their real beauty, though, lies in the fact that they're so versatile. With no particular specified space, they can move from room to room with ease. From the smallest two-drawer chest, just the right height to pull up next to a sofa or chair, to the tallest highboy, a focal-point piece equally appropriate for the bedroom or the dining room, these storage options make more sense than ever in today's mix-and-match society.

To get the most flexibility from a chest, make sure that its styling is simple and understated. A classic form with minimal ornamentation invariably has the most chameleon-like quality, making it right at home almost anywhere.

▲ BECAUSE THERE ARE NO SHARP CORNERS for passers-by to catch their clothing on, this arc-shaped demilune chest is particularly appropriate for an entry. The enclosed storage space holds last-minute essentials that you need before going out the door.

◀ FRENCH PROVINCIAL FURNISHINGS keep decoration to a minimum and yet still make a statement. This simple form is interrupted only by slightly stepped drawers and a gracefully carved base. The most elaborate of all is the hardware; its scrolling complements the ornamental lamp above.

▲ SET IN A BEDROOM, this chest accommodates folded clothing and provides three small setback drawers, just the right size for small change or jewelry. Although the pastoral painting reflects the traditional tone of the room, this chest could also be paired with a mirror and put in an entryway.

About Chest Styles

BY DEFINITION, A CHEST IS A PIECE OF FURNITURE that features multiple drawers. There's a wide variety of translations, although the most popular ones have traditional eighteenth-century roots.

- Bachelor's chest: Typically has two small drawers on top and three larger ones below. Today the term refers to any small chest of drawers.
- Demilune chest: Features a curved front that forms an arc or half circle. Its back is flat so that it can be set against a wall.
- Lowboy: Characterized by one or two narrow tiers of drawers. It is a chest of drawers set on legs.
- Highboy: Formed by placing an additional set of drawers on top of a lowboy and adding a decorative pediment.

Bathroom Vanities

IT USED TO BE THAT FINE FURNITURE was at home anywhere but the bath. Today, however, storage pieces appear in every room of the house—including the bathroom. The most popular form is the cabinet-turned-vanity. Manufacturers offer a variety of styles, ready for the sink and faucets of your choice to be dropped into the top. To create a one-of-a-kind piece, any cabinet can be transformed into a custom bath vanity. Just cut out the appropriate holes for the fixtures and make sure there's sufficient space for the plumbing below. Give some attention to the top, as well. If you don't add a hard surface such as tile be sure that you use a water sealer.

▼ THE DARK WOOD FINISH OF THIS VANITY grounds the decor in this master bathroom by balancing the pattern created by mosaic tiles. Centered in front of a large window, the piece's mirror echoes the gentle curve of the frosted glass.

▲ OUTFITTED WITH A SINGLE SINK, a small chest is a good choice for this powder room. To create more visual space in smaller bathrooms, install a vanity with legs. The area beneath it will add a feeling of openness to the room.

▲ SET BETWEEN A PAIR of stationary curtain panels, this white-painted chest continues the color established by the shade directly above it. As a result, the room appears taller in the process by encouraging the eye to move directly from floor to ceiling.

▼ FLANKED BY SHIELD-BACK CHAIRS, this bachelor's chest is already a stunning focal point, but it gets more attention by being placed on a contemporary checkerboard floor. The black and white tiles emphasize the traditional storage piece by leading the eye to it.

Armoires

I**T'S NO COINCIDENCE** that the term *armoire* is similar to the word *armor*. In fact, armoires were originally designed to store suits of metal. Although their original purpose no longer exists, providing storage is still their primary function. Today, armoires are used to store clothing in the bedroom, house linens in the bathroom, or hold dinnerware in the dining room. Likewise, in this age of electronics, they also accommodate home entertainment equipment in the family room.

While many of today's armoires are massive, much like the original designs, just as many are slim and trim, appropriate for smaller spaces. They also vary greatly in height, allowing you to choose one that fulfills your storage needs while comfortably fitting into a room, whether you want it to blend into the background or take a place of prominence.

▼ ALTHOUGH THIS ORIENTAL-STYLE ARMOIRE IS PETITE, it's still large enough to house a television set and DVD equipment. Small holes in the back of the piece allow cords to be plugged into a nearby electrical outlet.

▼ A PAINTED PIECE OF FURNITURE can provide a room with an instant focal point, particularly if the backdrop is kept in quiet, neutral colors. The softly draped walls contrast the armoire's antiqued finish, making it even more outstanding.

▲ EVEN IN A ROOM WITH AN EXTRA-HIGH CEILING you don't need an extra-tall armoire as long as you create the illusion. With its dark color, this one takes on a more massive appearance. A fan-like architectural element in the same hue gives the piece an even greater sense of height.

Home Office Armoires

NOT EVERYONE HAS THE LUXURY of dedicating a separate room to a home office. But that doesn't mean that you have to settle for spreading your paperwork all over the dining room table, either. With a single piece of furniture, you can organize your entire office and still be able to shut the door on it at the end of the day. An armoire specifically outfitted for office use includes more than a work surface. Today's versions also incorporate enough space for a computer monitor and hard drive as well as a pullout keyboard tray. There's sufficient room for files and a printer, too, not to mention cubbyholes for everything from pencils to paperclips.

The accompanying chair can be a conventional office style or decorative. Whichever you choose, be sure that it's on casters so that you can move it back and forth easily. When not in use, it can simply take its place alongside the armoire.

▲ MAKING THE HOME OFFICE ARMOIRE even more self-sufficient, today's pieces come with their own electrical outlets, allowing you to keep the conglomeration of cords within the armoire itself. When guests arrive, you can simply close the doors and hide the work space entirely.

Entertainment Centers

I F YOU NEED A PLACE FOR A MINIMAL NUMBER of home electronics, a TV cabinet or small armoire may be the best solution. On the other hand, if you have a large collection of entertainment equipment, a modular storage system may be the answer. You'll find units that can accommodate conventional TVs as well as flat screens and home theaters. Plus, there's room for DVD players and game-boxes; matching units that with open and closed storage provide even more practicality.

If you're the cutting-edge type, there are even entertainment units that incorporate plasma TVs that pop up out of the piece. Last but not least, built-ins are another option. Made to suit a precise space—and the exact dimensions of your electronics—built-ins are more expensive but add architectural interest, too. Whether you choose freestanding furniture or custom-made pieces, entertainment centers offer a wealth of opportunities.

▲ THE SIMPLICITY OF THIS FAMILY ROOM calls for an equally uncomplicated entertainment center. At the far end of the room, a floor-to-ceiling library visually balances the large storage piece; had it been a blank wall, the entertainment unit would have seemed too big for the space.

▲ THIS IMPRESSIVE WALL OF BUILT-IN STORAGE stretches from wall to wall, concealing entertainment equipment behind the center doors. The paneled doors and arch-topped shelves create a look that's unmistakably English.

▲ THERE'S DISPLAY SPACE and concealed storage in this entertainment unit. Treasured collectibles can be seen clearly through the glass door on the left, but the DVDs, videos, and all kinds of TV-related items are hidden below. When not in use, a door swings around to disguise the TV, too.

Sizing Up Your Entertainment Needs

BEFORE PURCHASING A HOME ENTERTAINMENT CENTER, take stock of the electronics that you have. Make a list of the components themselves as well as their dimensions. The list should include your television, VCR, DVD, speakers—anything that takes up physical space. Next, compile all of your CDs, DVDs, and video tapes and measure them to find out how much linear space they require. Once you've come up with a number, estimate how much more space you'll need as your collection grows. Only after you've done the math will you be ready to shop wisely for a new storage unit.

Dressers and Nightstands

TRIPLE DRESSERS HAVE BEEN A STAPLE in terms of bedroom storage for a long time. With three small drawers along the top tier and larger drawers on the bottom, they provide a good his and hers solution. They measure approximately 76 in. long, so there's room to share. What's more, the mirror that typically spans the width is practical while the reflection it creates adds a sense of spaciousness to a room. Or opt for a pair of matching bachelor's chests that are about half as wide. Place them side by side and top each with its own wall-hung mirror; a round one will provide a welcome contrast to the more angular storage unit. The advantage is that these chests—and mirrors—can later be moved for use in other rooms.

Nightstands provide another good opportunity for storage, both inside and out. Most popular is the two-drawer model that has adequate tabletop space. Small dressers can also serve at bedside as long as they're no more than 2 in. higher or lower than the top of the mattress.

Quality Checkpoints for Drawers

DRAWERS ARE THE CORE of any good storage piece. Before buying, check for these indicators of good quality:

- Dovetail joints in drawers: **Those that are nailed, screwed, or glued are not as stable.**
- Drawers that open and close easily with one hand: **Most quality pieces will have center glides, keeping them from wobbling from side to side. Drawer stops are important, too, to keep the drawer from coming all the way out when you open it.**
- Smooth, well-sanded interiors: **Rough surfaces are more likely to snag items such as clothing.**

NESTLED BETWEEN TWO WINDOWS in the reading area of this bedroom, a vintage-looking dresser provides tabletop space for lamps, favorite photos, and other personal treasures. It proves that a piece often thought of as purely practical can be eye catching, too.

▶ WHEN SPACE IS AT A PREMIUM, a single dresser can serve twin beds. This low, two-drawer version has enough surface space to accommodate both sleepers. A model ship sets a nautical tone here, but a reading lamp could just as easily stand in its place.

◀ THIS NIGHTSTAND IS EFFICIENT IN MORE WAYS THAN ONE. It provides storage space and a place for bedside necessities while its placement between the bed and the window wall allows for adequate room to make the bed each morning.

China Cabinets

SELECTING THE RIGHT CHINA CABINET is much like picking the right entertainment center. Before you can make a wise choice, you need to know precisely what will be housed within. Take inventory of your dinnerware, allowing for those pieces that you still want to purchase. Be sure to include china, silverware, stemware, and serving pieces. Table linens should be on the list, too, if you plan to put them in drawers or on shelves behind doors.

Most china cabinets feature completely enclosed storage, an important point unless you like to dust—or wash—your dinnerware on a regular basis. Many formal styles also incorporate interior lighting, allowing you to showcase your best pieces. Some of these lights are operated with simple switches while other cabinets are outfitted with special hinges that provide stepped-up levels of interior light with nothing more than a mere touch.

▼ REACHING NEARLY AS HIGH AS THE RAFTERS, the height of this china cabinet provides a more than average amount of storage. Because the cabinet's wood tone matches that of the beams, your eye connects the two and then travels to the vaulted ceiling, making the generously sized room appear even more spacious.

▲ THE LIGHT WOOD OF THIS CHINA CABINET nearly matches the hardwood floor. Both get more attention, though, next to the vibrant blue walls. Even the blue and white dinnerware seems to sparkle more brightly in the setting.

▲ AN ANTIQUE CUPBOARD SETTLES INTO A NICHE between the pantry and refrigerator in this kitchen. The niche may have been a pantry at one time but closet doors and shelves are easily removed to make room for a free-standing piece of furniture.

Quality Checkpoints for Doors

DOORS ARE MORE THAN MERE GUISES for the contents behind them. A quality door can enhance a storage piece while an ill-fitting one can quickly detract. Here's what to look for:

- Doors that hang evenly and swing with ease: Latches should also operate smoothly.
- Hinges that are firmly attached: Exterior hinges should have screws that go all the way through the door as well as the furniture frame, preferably anchored with a nut on the opposite side.

Sideboards and Buffets

BUFFETS, SIDEBOARDS, AND EVEN HUNTBOARDS all have the same basic size and shape as well as a common purpose. That is, they provide dining room storage space as well as serving areas. Only the huntboard is typically taller; that's because it was originally designed to serve hunters who had spent the day on horseback and preferred to stand while dining. Some of these serving pieces rest on delicate cabriole legs, while others are solid with storage reaching all the way to the floor. While personal preference should take precedence, keep in mind that leggy styles take up less visual space, sometimes an issue in a room with a large table and chairs plus a china cabinet.

Many of today's models are perfectly appropriate for other rooms, too. A sideboard, for instance, can be a good fit in the family room—its storage space can be used for games and photo albums, and the serving area is suitable for a casual buffet. It can also be used in the entryway for storage and a convenient drop-off spot.

▲ SQUARED PIECES OF VENEER on this modern buffet communicate a geometric theme. A small mirror propped against a wall-hung version further adds to the theme. The black-framed mirror is duplicated on the opposite wall, allowing for an endless reflection of geometric shapes.

◄ ALTHOUGH ITS DESIGN IS CENTURIES OLD, this traditional huntboard gets a modern-day twist. A black-and-white checkerboard floor gives it some contemporary flair while all-white accessories on top of the piece—including an arched window-turned-work of art—carry out the fresh approach.

▲ A SLIM BUFFET FITS PERFECTLY IN NARROW PASSAGEWAYS THROUGH ROOMS. This one makes up in style what it gives up in size. The red finish and paneled doors draw the eye, especially since the piece is set against a much-lighter wall.

Display Units

FOR THOSE WITH A PENCHANT FOR COLLECTIBLES, furnishings that display their objects are essential. The kind of unit you choose depends not only on where it will be placed but also on whether the display items are large or small, fragile or not. Curio cabinets, for instance, are a good way to display figurines because glass doors keep the collectibles safely away from curiosity-seekers and, at the same time, keep out dust. On the other hand, open-shelved pieces such as tall etageres allow easy access. And don't forget about baker's racks. Originally designed so bakers could display their day's bounty, the first baker's racks featured wire shelves that allowed the bread to cool. Today's adaptations, suitable for any informal room, have solid wood shelves that are more practical.

▼ CORNER CUPBOARDS ARE TYPICALLY FOUND in the dining room, displaying dinnerware on the open shelves and providing enclosed storage beneath. This one has found a new home in the nursery, where items that need to stay out of baby's reach are safely displayed.

▲ WITHIN EACH SHALLOW COMPARTMENT of this red-painted shelving unit, carefully chosen collectibles are equally outstanding. They co-exist peacefully because of their common vintage theme, and because each individual grouping is approximately the same size, there's a soothing sense of symmetry.

▲ COMPARTMENTALIZED SHELVES BUILT INTO THIS KITCHEN ISLAND serve a twofold purpose. Dishes and serving pieces are artfully arranged, adding a splash of color to this all-white kitchen. At the same time, they're easily accessible for mealtime.

Freestanding Storage

▲ A MIX OF OPEN AND CLOSED STORAGE is important in any child's room. The former displays favorite items while the latter keeps clothing tucked away neatly. This piece goes one step further by incorporating toy boxes. Set on casters, they move back and forth easily.

FREESTANDING STORAGE ENCOMPASSES PIECES LARGE AND SMALL, used anywhere throughout the house. Some may sit discreetly in a corner of a room while others just about touch the ceiling, a good solution when you're looking for storage space and there's nowhere to go but up. Some pieces even provide two-sided storage while others have backs that are finished well enough to make them handsome room dividers.

The best thing that freestanding storage pieces have going for them is that they're versatile. Not only can they be used to stash a wide variety of items but many can also move from room to room with ease. As a result, these kinds of furnishings provide some of the best buys for your decorating dollar.

▲ A TWO-TIERED BASKET ONCE USED AS A PLANT STAND now keeps fresh towels close to the tub in this bathroom. Because the lightweight storage piece has its own handle, it can easily be moved into a corner, out of the way.

QUICK FIX

Innovative Storage

FINDING ENOUGH STORAGE SPACE requires creativity. Here's how to discover extra room:

- Take advantage of wasted space behind doors. In the kitchen, attach a rack for aluminum foil and waxed paper behind the pantry door. In a bedroom closet, hang a shoe rack, and in a home office, fasten a wall grid that will hold file folders.
- Convert a closet into a home office or entertainment center. When not in use, close the doors to hide the equipment.
- Take a look at under-the-stairs space. It may provide the perfect place for the family computer or an entire library of books.

▲ THIS STAINLESS-STEEL CABINET conveys a vintage feel. The metal is easy to clean, an important point in a piece of kitchen furniture. Between upper and lower storage, the countertop can just as easily be used as a work area as it can display space.

▲ ADD A SIMPLE STORAGE UNIT TO A BATHROOM THAT DOESN'T HAVE A LINEN CLOSET. Here, a statuesque piece balances a sink and mirror combination. There's plenty of room for both storage and display, but glass-fronted doors let you see where everything is located.

Built-Ins

WHILE BUILT-INS DON'T AFFORD THE LUXURY OF MOVING with you from place to place, they have the advantage of being able to use every inch of potential storage space. They also provide the opportunity to create niches and nooks from floor to ceiling, spanning an entire wall, if you like. Or they can be incorporated into existing niches and nooks. A window seat, for instance, can lift up to reveal the perfect place for books and blankets. Nobody but you will ever be aware that the storage is there.

The benefit of built-ins is that they can be custom-tailored to your specific needs. There's more expense involved, but it may be worth it, literally, when it's time to sell your home; built-ins can be an attractive selling point. More often than not, though, you'll need the assistance of a professional—a contractor and, perhaps, a designer, too—to carry out the master plan.

▲ THIS BUILT-IN STORAGE UNIT creates its own visual interest with the careful placement of cabinetry. In the center, a pair of glass-front doors almost takes on the appearance of a window while, at either end, cabinets placed on an angle add even more architectural appeal.

▼ MUDROOMS OFTEN BECOME a conglomeration of coats and boots. This one solves that problem with built-in storage that gives each member of the family his or her own space. The open storage areas make things easy to grab and just as easy to put away.

▲ TOO OFTEN, UNDER-THE-STAIRS SPACE is simply wasted. That's not the case here; open and closed storage tucks neatly under the steps. It's an especially good spot for toys and games since it's easily accessible by anybody.

◄ THIS BEDROOM DOESN'T SETTLE for a mere nautical ambience. It takes a cue from a ship's storage solutions, too. Two drawers are built in under the bed, convenient for extra blankets or off-season clothing, while a small built-in chest optimizes space between the foot of the bed and the wall.

▲ IN THIS KITCHEN, a pair of conventional cupboard doors was removed to make way for a custom storage insert. Made out of light maple, it provides a warm contrast to the cool green cabinetry.

◄ ▲ TAKING ADVANTAGE OF A LITTLE-USED CORNER, this floor-to-ceiling storage unit has a stepped-back center section that incorporates a microwave, a small work area, and enclosed upper and lower storage. On each side, though, tall doors pull out to reveal storage for pantry items.

QUICK FIX

Replacing Knobs and Pulls

WITH LITTLE INVESTMENT, and even less time, doors and drawers can get an entirely different look with new hardware. Conventional knobs and pulls have a lot of competition today. There are glass versions with a vintage look, ceramics that replicate sailboats or other novelties, and even metal renditions made to look like leaves. Choose a style to match the mood of your room or mix things up—ceramic knobs in a variety of bright colors can add a playful touch to a child's room.

Before purchasing replacement knobs, do a little homework. Check to see whether the knobs that you'll be replacing require one or two screws. The former is typically considered a knob, whereas the latter is referred to as a pull. If you're replacing a knob, make sure that the new hardware is fitted with a screw similar in size to the one you have now. If necessary, you can make the hole in the door or drawer larger, but you can't make it smaller. In addition, if you're looking for new pulls, measure the distance between the holes to make sure the replacement piece will fit.

▲ ALTHOUGH EACH OF THE DOOR PULLS, above and below the basketry, is slightly different, they all work together beautifully because they're all made of wrought iron and have similar heft.

▲ THE SMALLEST SLIVER OF SPACE can pay big dividends in terms of storage. A niche was carved out in this bath, sectioned off and then tiled to match the rest of the room. The lower shelves are large enough to accommodate a pair of hampers.

◄ DRAWER STORAGE KEEPS UTENSILS close at hand, while a door opens to expose pantry items in this hard-working kitchen unit. An organizer on the back side of the door provides additional storage space. Most ingenious, though, is the drop-down door that conceals a wastebasket.

▲ A CABINET BUILT ATOP A MARBLE countertop maximizes storage in this bathroom by adding four levels of vertical space. Its glass doors allow you to see the contents within as well as the back of the cabinetry, which creates a greater sense of visual space.

▼ TO CARRY OUT THE ARTS AND CRAFTS STYLE OF THIS HOUSE, a Craftsman-style cabinet built of quartersawn oak stores bathroom toiletries behind its doors while open shelves keep fresh towels close at hand.

HOME OFFICES

▼ THE WINDOW IN THIS HOME OFFICE DIDN'T STAND IN THE WAY of creating an L-shaped storage wall. Because the shade matches the wall color and is close in tone to the built-in storage wall, the window becomes an integral part of the design.

► IN A HOME OFFICE THAT REQUIRES an extensive library, built-in shelves are the best option. Here, a series of squared-off shelves is interrupted by a row of drawers, placed at an easily accessible height. Below each drawer, a pullout tray provides a momentary reading surface.

Organize with Baskets and Bins

SHELF STORAGE IS EVERYWHERE YOU LOOK—in closets, kitchen pantries, and all kinds of cabinetry. But you can stack things just so high before they topple over. To keep that from happening, and still take advantage of every square inch, outfit your shelves with baskets and bins. Not only will they allow you to store more but you'll get more organized in the process.

Baskets are a natural for many spaces. In a family room, they can give a sense of order to everything from CDs and DVDs to toys and games. Likewise, they can tidy up a kitchen pantry. Devote one basket each to canned goods, pastas, and sauces, all the way down to spices and seasonings. Put a label on the front of each for immediate identification.

See-through plastic bins can also help keep your house in order. Use them in a closet to store shoes and sweaters or in a child's room for toys and games.

▲ THIS HOME OFFICE, TUCKED INTO A FORMER CLOSET, makes good use of every inch. Because the shelves reach to the ceiling, office essentials are corralled in baskets that are easy to take down; the least-used items are placed at the top.

▲ WINDOW SEATS OFTEN LIFT UP to reveal hidden storage beneath. This example, however, takes convenience to another level. Directly beneath the padded seat, a single shelf holds reference books. Because the shelf is at floor level, there is adequate support for the weight of the books.

Lighting

A balanced approach is the key to any well-lit room. In a dining room, this means more than a chandelier over the table. And it's more than a reading lamp in the bedroom. Each room requires three types of lighting—ambient, task, and accent. With the right combination, there's sufficient illumination at all levels; you can see your way from one room to the next, read a book or follow a recipe, or even draw attention to a special work of art.

The beauty (literally) of this three-prong approach is that it provides visual excitement, too. With a variety of lamps at eye level, wall sconces a little higher, and fixtures overhead, a well-balanced lighting plan creates light and dark areas that spotlight some items and leave others subtly in the shadows. When putting your plan together, though, keep in mind what time of day you will use the room most. Formal living and dining rooms, for instance, are most often used during the evening hours. That may mean you'll want to turn up the wattage to keep guests from sitting in the dark. The choice is yours, though. With the right lighting scheme, a room can be brilliant or dimly dramatic.

◀ SIDE-BY-SIDE PENDANT LIGHTS OVER THE ISLAND IN THIS KITCHEN are hung low enough to give the cook adequate light when chopping fruits and vegetables on the butcher-block top. Made of copper, these fixtures have an artistic flair, too, in keeping with the rest of the room.

Ambient Lighting

ON ITS MOST BASIC LEVEL, ambient (or general) lighting allows a person to walk safely through a room. It keeps you from stepping on the cat, stubbing your toe, or slipping on a wet surface. Beyond that, however, ambient lighting gives a room a soft, overall glow. It also provides a support system for task and accent lighting. Once a room's ambient lighting is in place, you can concentrate on illuminating specific surfaces and areas.

One of the best sources of general illumination is recessed lighting, in which spotlights are placed evenly throughout a room. Track lighting is another good choice because you can position its moveable fixtures to create a comfortable overall ambience. Whatever type of lighting you choose, make sure that it's evenly distributed. But don't feel that you're locked into a certain level of brightness. By using a simple dimmer switch you can raise or lower the light level quickly.

▲ TABLE LAMPS ARE AN EASY WAY to brighten the corners of a room, areas that have a natural tendency to be dark. This contemporary lamp sheds light on a bay, its base echoing the same warm finish of the table it's set on.

◄ THE FIXTURES WITHIN A ROOM need not all be the same. In this space, small but intense lights are on the same track with more decorative pendants. The benefit of track systems is that they're flexible, allowing you to shine light where it's needed most.

PENDANT LAMPS PROVIDE TASK LIGHTING over the island of this kitchen as well as the dining area. Strategically placed recessed lights— in front of the refrigerator and pantry and over the far work surface—also illuminate the tasks at hand while ambient uplights bring out the warmth of the wood ceiling.

A PAIR OF METAL PENDANTS, lined in brass to cast a warm glow, spread even light over this dining area. The twosome is in keeping with the symmetrical design of the space. Their round shapes also echo the circular shapes of the chair backs.

▼ OVERHEAD FIXTURES ARE ESSENTIAL IN A FRONT HALL, but lighting on another level can provide added assistance. Atop this console table, a pair of lamps supply general illumination but also cast enough light for a last-minute appearance check in the mirror.

▲ LIKE ANY OTHER DECORATIVE ELEMENT, a chandelier needs to be the right size and scale for the space that it's in. This one is large enough to suit the grand entrance hall and hung low enough so that it sheds light on the foyer below.

▼ A FROSTED GLASS CEILING FIXTURE supplies this entryway with soft ambient lighting. The bottom of the light is level with the tops of the doors, so there's no danger of hitting your head. Meanwhile, a nearby table lamp provides task lighting while adding an artistic touch.

Spacing Light Fixtures

THE NUMBER OF LIGHT FIXTURES needed in a stairway or hall depends not only on the fixtures you're using but also how far apart they'll be placed. Pairs of wall sconces positioned on both sides of a hallway can be installed up to 12 ft. apart. When sconces are used on only one wall—along a stairway, for instance—or when they are fitted with low-wattage bulbs, they should be closer together. The goal is to have the entire length of the space fully lit with few shadows.

▲ INDIRECT LIGHTING, IN THE FORM OF COVE LIGHTS, reflects light off of the ceiling and back down to the floor. It's a strategy that works particularly well here since white, used on the ceiling, the extensive trim work, and the floor, is a good reflector.

NO LONGER RESERVED FOR TABLE LAMPS, drum shades have become popular in pendant styles. This trio of lights, suspended from shiny brass rods, illuminates the dining space below. The fixtures' cylindrical shapes counterbalance the sharp edges of the table and chairs.

TRICKS OF THE TRADE

Add a Dimmer Switch

A DIMMER SWITCH IS ONE OF THE EASIEST and least expensive ways to add drama to a room. They've long been used in the dining room but are now appearing in the kitchen, the powder room, even the master bedroom. To ensure that your light is a candidate for a dimmer switch, check the back of the dimmer package. Generally, fluorescent lights and halogens are not good options nor are three-way switches. Dimmers are available in toggle and dial styles; some are even touch-sensitive. Be sure to select one that's rated to handle the total wattage of the lights it will control.

▲ A PENDANT LAMP SHINES OVER THIS DINING TABLE, but the ambient lighting in this room gets a boost from a pair of lamps on the sideboard. Decorative bases pick up the color of the chairs while drum shades are intentionally short to keep the attention focused on the lamp bases.

▲ TO SPREAD SUFFICIENT LIGHT over the entire dining table, this pendant lamp is hung a bit higher than usual. The splayed shape of the fixture allows the light to shine in a larger-diameter pattern the closer it is to the ceiling.

◄ FIXTURES SHOULD ECHO THE SHAPE of the dining table itself. A round table should have light that forms a circle, whereas fixtures over a rectangular table should echo its linear form. This wrought-iron chandelier follows that guideline, its gold-lined shades reflecting light downward onto the table.

About Light Bulbs

Today's light bulbs vary almost as much as the lighting fixtures they fit. Here are the three most common to choose from:

- **Incandescent:** Incandescents cast a warm, soft glow. They're appropriate for both ambient and task lighting.
- **Halogen:** Halogen bulbs provide clear white light. They are more energy efficient than incandescents, but the disadvantage is that they get very hot, creating a fire hazard.
- **Fluorescent:** The most efficient option around, today's fluorescent tubes match the warm glow of incandescents. They also come in a smaller size—compact fluorescent light bulbs (CFLs) fit into spaces designed for incandescent bulbs.

▲ CANDLELIGHT IS SOOTHING but doesn't provide sufficient illumination. This kitchen, though, gets the best of both worlds. A flat suspended surface holds what seem to be white pillars. But the fixture is actually electrified, allowing the light to shine through, providing ambient light but enough illumination for kitchen tasks, too.

▶ THE COLONIAL BLUE HUE OF THIS KITCHEN quickly identifies the space as traditional, but a pair of whimsical pendants doesn't allow it to become too serious. The globe-shaped fixtures complement the red cast-iron stove, creating a fresh color scheme of red, white, and blue.

▲ RECESSED LIGHTS THROUGHOUT THIS KITCHEN ensure overall illumination as well as task lighting. Meanwhile, the purely decorative fixture above the island is hung high to give it more importance. A lamp beside the sink casts a soft light, ideal for finding your way around the room for a midnight snack.

◄ WEIGHTED PENDANT LIGHTS over this kitchen island allow the fixtures to be pulled as close, or as far away, as desired. For general lighting, this raised position casts a soft glow on the surrounding area. When more focused light is required, the fixture can easily be lowered.

Task Lighting

TASK LIGHTING SHEDS LIGHT ON ACTIVITIES. Whether it's reading or writing, working on a craft project, or playing the piano, task lighting will make the job easier. As a rule, lighting fitted with soft white bulbs, as opposed to clear bulbs, is better because the light is easier on the eyes. To further control glare, use a three-way bulb or dimmer. It's also important that task lighting illuminate evenly; one side of the magazine you're reading should not be darker than the other.

Cone-shaped shades are one of the best options for task lighting as they provide a generous pool of light. If you choose a drum shade that has an opening at both top and bottom, it can serve double duty, shedding light on the intended task and reflecting light off the ceiling. Some shades have a different color inside than the outside; a crisp white shade, for instance, might have a pale pink interior, giving the light an even softer glow.

▲ EMPLOY FLOOR LAMPS when space is limited. Here, a chair-side table wasn't large enough to accommodate a table lamp, so a floor model was used. Its elbow and head are both adjustable, putting light precisely where it's needed most.

◄ ELONGATED PENDANT LIGHTS with frosted shades hang over the sinks in this master bathroom, providing ample light for tasks such as shaving and applying makeup. The mirror above the vanity reflects light back into the room, providing even brighter illumination.

▲ CONTEMPORARY ARCHITECTURE IN THIS BEDROOM CALLED FOR LIGHTING EQUALLY MODERN IN STYLE. At the same time, it needed to be understated, not competing with the custom headboard. These white gooseneck fixtures are the ideal choice because they blend quietly into the background.

Beyond Soft White Bulbs

OLOR IS ONE OF THE BEST WAYS to establish a room's mood. Whether you want a soothing cool scheme or something spicy and hot, painted walls and rich fabrics can help you achieve the desired effect. And now lighting is getting into the act. Soft pink incandescent bulbs have been available for some time, but the color craze has now jumped to an entirely new level. Transparent incandescents are now readily available in red, blue, yellow, and green; for longer-life bulbs, compact spiral fluorescents (which fit into standard sockets) can be found, too. And for the truly color courageous there's even turquoise, purple, and orange.

▶ A STORAGE WALL BUILT AROUND this bed does more than create a cozy refuge. The resulting sidewalls allow room for built-in niches—just big enough for family photos or an alarm clock—as well as adjustable-arm lamps, which can be easily positioned for bedtime reading.

Lamp shades come in a wide variety of styles, any of which can give a base a brand new look. It's helpful, though, to know what your options are and what to ask for at the store. Generally, a shade should be approximately two-thirds the height of the lamp base and about one and a half times the width. Here are some of the most familiar designs:

CONICAL

DRUM

HEXAGON

SQUARE

The Right Height

SUCCESSFUL LIGHTING **requires that the fixture be placed at the right height.**

- **Table and floor lamps:** It's important that table and floor lamps not be too high or too low. One with a shade that's too high will leave you starting at a bare bulb; one that's too low will shed a pool of light on the table or floor but little else. For general lighting, the bottom of a lamp's shade should be at eye level when someone is seated, approximately 38 in. to 42 in. from the floor. For reading or other tasks, the bottom of the shade should be approximately 12 in. below eye level.

- **Pendant lamps and chandeliers:** As a general rule, a pendant lamp or chandelier should be positioned so the bottom is approximately 30 in. above the surface that it illuminates, such as a table or countertop. When the height of the room is over 8 ft., though, raise the height 2 in. or 3 in. per extra foot for better visual balance.

- **Sconces:** The height of wall sconces is mostly a matter of personal preference. Typically, though, they are positioned at eye level.

▲ THE STYLE OF A LAMP'S BASE influences the choice of shade. The most important consideration when choosing a shade, though, is height: A shade should go from the lamp's finial to just below the bulb socket. This traditional two-handled urn called for something special like this intricately pleated design.

Accent Lighting

PURELY DECORATIVE, accent lighting adds drama to a room. It can be used to highlight a favorite painting or simply wash a wall with light. Spotlights and track lights are most commonly used as accents because their light can be precisely aimed at an object. Other sources include sconces and uplights—can-style fixtures set directly on the floor. But no matter what type of light is used, there is a single formula to follow: Accent lighting should be brighter than ambient lighting.

To accent a wall, perhaps one with a textured surface or bold color, use a row of track or recessed lights. Position them on the ceiling 2 ft. to 3 ft. from the wall. They should be angled in the same direction, allowing each fixture to bathe the wall in light. Similarly, a carefully placed uplight might cast light up into a house plant, giving it dramatic impact.

▼ INSTALLED WITHIN A DISPLAY UNIT, recessed lights draw the eye to cherished pieces of art. Here, a collection of art glass is called to attention by tightly focused beams. The interior shelves get the benefit, too, with light spilling onto the softly painted walls.

▲ THIS PAIR OF BRASS SCONCES SUPPLEMENTS THE ROOM'S AMBIENT LIGHTING and, when turned on, call attention to the focal point wall. All alone, they provide intimate additional lighting for a candlelit dinner.

▲ IN AN ENTRY HALL where geometric shapes predominate, a pair of shapely sconces is a welcome change of pace. The overall height of the light fixtures is in keeping with the space's tall ceiling. But more important, the sconces bring a source of light down to eye level.

A TORCHERE—THE FRENCH WORD FOR "CANDLESTAND"—has a similar appearance to its translated name. Here, the tall uplight, with a bell-shaped shade, casts light toward the ceiling, drawing the eye in the same direction and in the process making the room seem taller.

GIVING THE IMPRESSION OF LIGHTS WITHIN A LIGHT, this accent piece features a harlequin-robed figure carrying a pair of mini-lanterns. The piece could stand as a decorative accessory on its own, but the addition of light makes it even more eye catching.

On the Right Track

TRACK LIGHTING HAS LONG BEEN the most flexible type of illumination in the house. The lights mounted along a track can be changed and rearranged, added or deleted. Today, you can even change the type of light entirely or use a mix of styles along a single track: You may want to use can lights that are specifically directed at objects such as artwork and then add a pair of pendants for ambient lighting. The way in which track lights are attached, too, is ever changing. For starters, the track itself is no longer always perfectly straight; some tracks have enough flexibility that they can be curved to follow any line you establish. Plus, not all lights need to be attached directly to the track itself. Some lightweight models are suspended from their tracks with nothing more than thin wire.

There are two types of track lighting. One system has a cord that is simply plugged into an existing outlet; it doesn't require any special wiring but it does need to be located near an outlet. The second type has no exposed wiring; instead, electrical connections must be made at an electrical junction box in the ceiling or wall.

▲ AT FIRST GLANCE, THE TRACK LIGHTS IN THIS FAMILY ROOM appear to be providing general lighting. To a certain extent that's true, but it's apparent on closer inspection that they primarily spotlight specific pieces such as the sectional sofa and the pool table.

◀ A DECORATIVE LAMP casts a soft glow on this tablescape, but it's a small picture light, attached to the oil painting above, that makes the artwork the undisputed focal point of this traditional grouping.

Decorative Accessories

Putting the finishing touches on a room is no different from accessorizing an outfit—even with the best basics in place, an outfit doesn't truly shine without accessories. Think of the little black dress, for instance, without the strand of pearls. It's a good look but has the potential of being so much better.

Decorating takes the same approach as fashion: Just a few carefully selected accessories can turn an ordinary room into something extraordinary. What's more, it's the single best way to play up your personality. Are you steeped in tradition? If so, serious artwork may grace your walls. Or, if you're more free-spirited, put fun and funky collectibles prominently on display.

Decorative accessories throughout your house need not be of the same vintage, either. In fact, it's much more interesting to mix old and new, fine objects with found items, hand-me-downs with newly purchased pieces. From time to time, too, change your perspective by changing and rearranging things. Go "shopping" in your own home, looking in all-but-forgotten boxes in the basement or attic. You'll be surprised by the number of treasures you'll find that blend beautifully into your scheme.

◄ ALTHOUGH THESE FOUR PRINTS HAVE SIMILAR SUBJECT MATTER, they're made even more compatible by the identical white mats and black frames. By grouping the quartet closely together, too, it gives the viewer a single focus and makes a more dramatic statement.

Wall Art

WE'RE LONG PAST THE DAY when wall art consisted solely of paintings, posters, or prints. Today, we're more inclined to let our imaginations run wild, including anything that can be supported by a nail in the wall. From decorative plates to architectural elements—even store signs, boat oars, or a criss-crossed pair of skis—wall art truly is in the eye of the beholder.

And what if the objects of your desire aren't conducive to being hung on the wall? There's often a way to get around that; small items such as pottery and figurines fit neatly on wall-hung shelves. Use one alone, stack several like bookshelves, or make them a part of a larger grouping. You'll find that their flexibility knows no bounds.

▶ ROUGH-HEWN WALL BRACKETS provide an interesting counterpoint to the high sheen of the decoupaged plates that they support. Set on stands atop the individual brackets, the plates take on more of a three-dimensional feeling.

▼ A PAIR OF VICTORIAN SCREEN DOORS may have outlived their original purpose but in this dining area, they get a new lease on life as one-of-a-kind artwork. Their scrolling motifs add a welcome touch of softness to the straightforward wood paneling.

▼ PROVING THAT YOU CAN HAVE IT ALL, this wall grouping incorporates decorative plates, collectibles on wall brackets, and four gold-framed prints. The symmetrical arrangement is no coincidence, either; it allows each piece to stand out prominently.

PICTURES AND PRINTS

▲ FRAMED IN A BRILLIANT SHADE OF ORANGE, this group of contemporary prints makes you wonder: Did the room's color palette inspire the frames or vice versa? Either way, it speaks to the fact that frames don't have to be the conventional gold or wood options.

▲ THREE CONTEMPORARY PRINTS ARE STACKED VERTICALLY in this living room, leading the eye right up to the soaring ceiling. The dark wood frames further emphasize this architectural asset, standing out prominently against the orange painted backdrop.

▲ THIS TRIO OF COLORFUL PAINTINGS emphasizes the horizontal lines of the bed's headboard—as well as the transom windows and their small square counterparts throughout the room. Set against the white walls of this high-ceilinged space, they also keep the eye at a lower level, creating a sense of intimacy.

► THIS ASSORTMENT OF PICTURES AND PRINTS features frames that range from traditional gold to more contemporary acrylic. It's the subject matter, though, that provides the thread of continuity; everything here is in black and white. Burnt orange walls bring just the right touch of warmth to the setting.

Getting the Hang of It

OMPOSING A WALL GROUPING doesn't have to be difficult. Start with a piece of kraft paper (found at a local art supply store) large enough to contain your finished grouping. Put it on the floor, and then arrange the elements you're using. Position the pieces so there is one strong horizontal line. You may want to incorporate a strong vertical line, too. Keep moving the items around, balancing heavy and light (from physical and visual points of view). You may want to keep the spacing between pieces equidistant; by doing so, the group will hang together better as a whole.

Once you're satisfied, mark where the nail holes should be for each piece. Then, with painter's tape, attach the kraft paper to the wall. (For a behind-the-sofa grouping, hang the bottom pieces low enough so there's a visual link to the piece of furniture, but not so low that you'll hit your head against them.) Drive nails and/or hangers into the appropriate places, and then remove the paper from the wall. (If wall anchors are needed, determine their positions on the paper but don't install them until after the paper's been removed.) Finally, put each piece of wall art in its predetermined spot.

◄ GROUPING ARTWORK of varying sizes is easier when there is a common element, whether it's similar colors, frames, or subjects—like these contemporary examples. So that the eye has something to focus on, groupings should generally form a geometric shape such as a square or rectangle.

▲ ART DOESN'T HAVE TO BE HUNG ON THE WALL. The mirrors in this dressing room embellish the fronts of storage doors. Suspended with ribbon, it's a look that can be applied to any wall-hung art, using ribbon, rope, and even colorful twine.

◄ WHEN IT COMES TO SMALL SPACES, simplicity is often the best approach. In this bathroom, delicate ferns in identical frames all but blend into the white wainscoting. To make sure that doesn't happen, though, a pair of slightly larger examples underscores the smaller set.

▲ A PIECE OF ART CAN BE GIVEN MORE IMPORTANCE with the right frame. The conventional gold frame is appropriate for this portrait; a more rustic piece of art would call for a primitive wood or painted style. Topiaries on either side of this piece provide a handsome secondary framework.

CREATIVE WALL ART

▼ TAKING A CUE FROM THE BLUE AND WHITE TOILE PATTERN in the bed dressings, decorative plates in the same two hues are arranged artistically over the headboard. While mimicking the gentle curves may have been expected, the angular placement provides an eye-pleasing counterpoint and serves as a "canopy" of sorts.

▲ SOMETIMES ALL IT TAKES IS A SINGLE ELEMENT to make a dramatic statement. In this room full of smooth surfaces— in the upholstered chair, the low bench, even the table lamp—an architectural element, with spokes seemingly radiating from the center, is a standout.

▲ ONE OF THE MOST IMPORTANT DESIGN PRINCIPLES, balance can be translated in many ways. The flat surface of this bench, for instance, is approached the same way as a mantel with asymmetrical style. A favorite work of art is balanced here by several smaller items.

◄ ALTHOUGH IT HAS A WIDE VARIETY OF ELEMENTS, this grouping is balanced beautifully. Over the bed and accompanying night table, a needlework sampler, wall-hung shelf, and vintage sign demonstrate asymmetrical balance. Meanwhile, atop the shelf, a clock and two figures are the epitome of symmetrical styling.

Collectibles

ACCESSORIES THAT FALL INTO THE COLLECTIBLES CATEGORY offer some of the best ways to express your personal style. They are, after all, pieces that you find yourself drawn to time after time. Why stash them away when you can share them with family and friends, making them a part of your decorating scheme in the process?

When displaying collectibles of any kind, it's important not to break up the set. Pieces grouped together make a greater impression than those spread throughout a room or throughout the house. Keep in mind, too, that an odd number of objects is more interesting than an even number, particularly if you're working with just a few items. The eye tends to "divide" even-numbered groupings in half—and doesn't know which half to look at first.

▲ THIS COLLECTION OF GLASSWARE includes a variety of shapes and sizes. A sense of balance exists, however. Because the two largest pieces are dark, they carry more visual weight. Three lighter pieces— with the help of a small dark one—keep them from becoming overpowering.

▲ A COLLECTIBLE FAVORED BY YOUNG AND OLD, snow globes quickly tell a story of where the owner has been. These are showcased particularly well; their black bases contrast with the table surface and light streaming through the windows allows the details of each to shine.

▶ ITEMS WITH COMMON COLORS or similar subject matter are always good candidates for groupings. Here, a collection of stainless-steel thermos bottles, shakers, and cups draw even more attention thanks to contrasting textures in the crackle-finished chest, the wood-paneled wall, even the galvanized bucket of flowers.

▲ A TESTAMENT TO A LOVE OF TRAVEL, this grouping is backed with three framed maps. The lampshade is a standout, too, not only because it's unusual, but also because it's teamed with a simple white base. Map-covered cubes bring the subject matter down to the tabletop.

Tablescaping

THE FIRST RULE OF ANY SUCCESSFUL TABLESCAPE—an arrangement on top of any flat surface—is that the number of items doesn't overwhelm the available space. A large collection of family photos works fine atop a grand piano but will likely crowd an end table.

Once you've determined the amount of space available, pare down items to an odd number; it will keep things from getting static, encouraging the eye to move from place to place. Then, play with the arrangement itself. No matter what kind of accessories you're working with—traditional, country, contemporary, even retro—an informal approach works best. Start by placing your tallest item at the back, set in slightly from one side or the other. Then, work your way forward gradually, ending with the smallest piece at the front of the area you're working with. For a well-balanced look, make sure that heights go up and down—from side to side and front to back. If too many items are similar in height, use small antique books to give them a lift.

Finally, don't cluster things too closely together. A little breathing room lets you better appreciate the merits of each piece.

▲ A VARIETY OF NATIVE AMERICAN–THEMED ACCESSORIES—from dolls to decorative boxes—create a one-of-a-kind tablescape atop this antique chest. The theme runs right up the walls, too, where a print and a souvenir-laden shelf unit solidly anchor the vignette.

▲ PERFECTLY APPROPRIATE FOR THIS SEASIDE HOME, a model boat, binoculars, and collected seashells make up this simple tablescape. It's the color of the fresh flowers, however, that brings your eye to the table; the fact that they can be changed seasonally allows the room's accent hue to change, too.

▲ WHEN IT COMES TO ACCESSORIZING, juxtaposition is everything. Here, an old wooden box is a surprising partner for a delicate white orchid. Likewise, a small set of binoculars is a functional addition while the string of colorful soda pop caps is just fun.

▼ GREEN KITCHENWARE, IN ALL SHAPES AND SIZES, **show** how a single color can unite disparate items. Corralled within a wall-hung storage unit—positioned slightly above the windows to create greater importance—these collectibles have a sense of stick-togetherness that is key to their success.

▲ ANTIQUE GAME BOARDS HUNG ALONGSIDE THIS STAIRWAY have a woven appearance like the runner itself. But the accessories don't stop there; baskets sit atop every other tread. Had they been displayed on a horizontal surface, the baskets—all of a similar height—would have gotten lost in the crowd.

▶ THIS COLLECTION OF PITCHERS AND JUGS indicates the owner's penchant for antiques. That supposition is played out in the accompanying wrought-iron candlesticks, and even the wall-hung print has a distinct aged appearance—all seemingly of the same era.

◄ FOUR CURVACEOUS VESSELS march across the top of this cabinet, stopped on the left side by a tall, rectangular piece propped against the wall. Its geometric shape, along with the grid-like architectural piece on the wall, provides a pleasing contrast for the shapely containers.

▼ A PLATE RACK FULL OF RED AND WHITE IRONSTONE provides a colorful focal point in this breakfast room. While the plates can be used on a daily basis, companion pieces—surrounding the rack on three sides—simply serve to make more of a decorative impact.

▲ THESE ANTIQUE PEWTER PIECES are silhouetted against a light, cream-color wall, allowing the shape of each piece to be appreciated. On the adjacent wall, more pewter—on a tabletop and some high shelves—blend quietly into the background but still balance the major collection.

Picture This!

AFTER SEVERAL ROUNDS OF **changing and rearranging, you've finally come up with the perfect tablescape.** The items are perfect, the balance is right—the design is working on every level. What happens, though, when cleaning day rolls around? Will you be able to replicate your arrangement? You will if you follow this trick: Once you're satisfied with your tablescape, take a picture of it. Keep it close at hand and you—or anyone else in the family—will be able to reproduce the look time after time.

▲ SO AS NOT TO COMPETE with the collectibles themselves, an unassuming display case is the perfect foil for this colorful Pez™ collection. What's more, it's a recycled piece—a drawer that's been given a glass-front door and a Pez handle, of course.

◄ A LATE NINETEENTH-CENTURY CUPBOARD IS THE PERFECT SHOWCASE for this collection of blue and white stoneware. The color combination even shows up in the storage piece itself; the creamy white exterior and blue-painted interior further strengthen the impact of these treasured pieces.

Mantels

WHEN IT COMES TO ACCESSORIZING A MANTEL, there's not a thing wrong with the proverbial picture over the fireplace, especially if it's a family portrait or if you are the featured artist. It's important to keep your options open, though, knowing that there are so many more alternatives.

Before you decide what kind of accessories to use, you'll need to determine how you want to approach the design. Do you want to create a soaring sense of height, perhaps in keeping with a room's cathedral ceiling? Or do you want to keep things more on eye level, creating a horizontal look that echoes the line of the mantel itself? There is no right or wrong; either tactic works in any room. It's purely a matter of personal preference.

▼ THIS GROUPING INCLUDES WALL-HUNG ACCESSORIES as well as pieces set on the mantel itself. The overall effect is horizontal—necessitated somewhat by the standard-height ceiling—yet there's subtle curvature along the top that gives it a more graceful feeling.

◀ A SAILBOAT HUNG above this fire-place is a clear indicator of the owner's passion for the sea. It also gives the flat wall three-dimensional interest. Meanwhile, a pair of smaller-scale models on the mantel below under-scores the larger version and further emphasizes the nautical theme.

▼ A MIRROR CENTERED OVER A MANTEL is a popular alternative to a painting or print; keep in mind, though, that a mirror should be positioned so that it reflects an area worth seeing twice. Here, flower stems in clear glass provide a subtle finishing touch.

Show Your Stuff

A FIREPLACE, AND THE MANTEL ABOVE IT, is typically the focal point of the room, and the perfect place to showcase treasured collectibles. A mantel provides plenty of space to display:

■ Colorful glass swizzle sticks, grouped by color or theme, corralled in a variety of glasses.

■ Mugs collected from places you've been, perhaps all in the same style, such as old-fashioned diner mugs.

■ Mirrors, propped against the wall, in a variety of sizes and frames.

■ A collection of metronomes that speaks to an interest in music.

► THE ORNATE MIRROR above this fireplace is the perfect companion for the intricately detailed mantel below. To bridge the gap between mantel and mirror, decorative plates flank each side, backed by tall floral arrangements. Two crystal sconces illuminate the display and add further balance.

◄ AN INTERESTING ALTERNATIVE to displaying decorative plates atop a mantel, this collection of blue and white pieces is hung on the wall directly above the architectural element. They follow the horizontal line but at each end turn upward to accentuate the decorative sconces.

Symmetrical vs. Asymmetrical Design

MANTEL ARRANGEMENTS usually fall into one of two categories. They either exhibit formal, symmetrical balance or its more informal, asymmetrical counterpart.

Symmetrical balance, as its name implies, is similar to mirror imagery. If you were to divide the wall above your mantel in half, each portion would be decorated exactly the same way. Most often used in traditional settings, symmetrical arrangements typically use objects that are identical. It's not a prerequisite, though, as long as the objects are similar enough to create the sense of a perfect match. While symmetrical balance is easy to achieve, it does have one

drawback: Perfectly matched items can sometimes cross that fine line, going from beautiful to boring.

Asymmetrical balance, on the other hand, refers to groupings characterized by an even distribution of size, or visual "weight." You might, for instance, have five decorative boxes stacked in a pyramid on one side of the mantel and a massive hurricane lamp on the other. They're entirely different elements but they carry the same visual weight. Asymmetrical arrangements are also likely to incorporate large and small items, short and tall, all the way across the mantle—leaving just a few open spots here and there to allow for breathing room.

▲ IN A LIVING ROOM THAT EXUDES CASUAL ELEGANCE, asymmetrical style provides a finishing touch. Atop the mantel, a vase of curly willow takes center stage. It's perfectly balanced on either side with two candle pillars on the left and a stout teapot on the right.

▲ THE EPITOME OF SYMMETRICAL STYLE, this arrangement is identical from side to side. It's elegant on its own but gets just the right touch of excitement from the painted cove moldings above that echo the color of the artwork, the sculpture, and the urns.

Soft Stuff

IN ANY WELL-DESIGNED ROOM, the difference is in the details, especially when it comes to the soft touches. A pillow here, a cozy throw there; they all add up to a sense of warmth—both figuratively and literally.

There's a proliferation of pillows available today, from highly decorative styles to those that all but make you laugh out loud. And there's an equally vast assortment of throws, woven in yarns so soft that you won't wait for a chill in the air before wrapping up in one. The same goes for bed linens, too. We've come a long way since the days of having a single bedspread; today, our beds have multiple dressings that make the bed even more of a focal point in the bedroom. The important thing to remember, in all cases, is to mix, don't match. You'll find that the results will be infinitely more interesting.

▲ SOMETIMES YOU ONLY NEED a whisper of color to add some visual interest. Here, a pale yellow and white pillow provides just the right amount of accent color for a stark white upholstered chair. It's so subtle, in fact, that the yellow accent becomes a neutral hue in its own right.

◄ YOU NEED NOT COMBINE countless colors and patterns to master the art of the mix. This bedroom intentionally keeps things low key, teaming blue and white quilted bed linens with a simple white ruffled bed skirt. Even the nearby bench is casually covered with a white throw.

▲ UPHOLSTERED IN A WHIMSICAL MIX OF FABRICS, this armchair sets the stage for patchwork pillows. The pillows repeat the navy and white hues of the chair and add a splash of red. Creating a perfect balance of primary colors are the yellow and white stripes.

▲ DRAPED CASUALLY OVER A WICKER CHAIR, this spring green and yellow plaid throw echoes the primary colors of the room without repeating a specific pattern. Just as important, it softens the look of the harder-edged wicker chair.

Credits

p. 4: Photo © davidduncanliving-ston.com; p. 5: Photo © Mark Samu, Design: EJR Architects.

CHAPTER 1

p. 6: Photo © davidduncanliving-ston.com; p. 7: Photo © Eric Roth; p. 8: (top) Photo © Mark Samu, Design: Sherrill Canet Design; (bottom) Photo © davidduncan-livingston.com; p. 9: Photo © Eric Roth, Design: Frank Roop; p. 10: (left) Photo © Mark Samu, Design: Sherrill Canet Design; (right) Photo © Rob Karosis/rob-karosis.com; p. 11: Photo © Jessie Walker; p. 12: (top) Photo © Mark Samu, Design: Hudson River Fine Interiors; (bottom) Photo © david-duncanlivingston. com; p. 13: Photo by Brian Vanden Brink, photographer © 2005, Design: Drysdale Associates Interior Designs; p. 14: Photo by Brian Vanden Brink, photographer © 2005, Design: Susan Thorn; p. 15: (top) Photo © Steve Vierra/ stevevierraphotography.com, Design: Beautiful Things; (bottom) Photo © Robert Perron, Design: Judith Griffins Interiors.

CHAPTER 2

p. 16: Photo © Jessie Walker, Design: The Cornerstone Studio, Wisconsin; p. 17: (left) Photo © Jessie Walker, Design: The Corner-stone Studio, Wisconsin; (middle) Photo © Eric Roth, Design: Susan Sargent; (right) Photo © david-duncanlivingston.com; p. 18: (top) Photo © Tim Street-Porter; (bot-tom) Photo © Eric Roth, Design: Susan Sargent; p. 19: Photo cour-tesy Harrison Design Associates; p. 20: (top) Photo © Eric Roth, Design: Deb Roub; (bottom) Photo © Rob Karosis/robkaro-sis.com, Design: James Coursey, Architecture: TMS Architects; p.21; (top) Photo © Steve Vierra/steve-vierraphotography.com, Design: Gary McBournie; (bottom) Photo © davidduncanlivingston.com; p. 22: (top) Photo © Steve Vierra/ stevevierraphotography.com, Design: Mary McGee; (bottom) Photo © Mark Samu, Design: Sherrill Canet Design; p. 23: Photo © davidduncanlivingston.com; p. 24: Photo © Mark Samu,

Design: Eileen Kathryn Boyd Inte-riors; p. 25: (top) Photo © Mark Samu, Design: Eileen Kathryn Boyd Interiors; (bottom) Photo courtesy of Harrison Design Asso-ciates; p. 26: (top left) Photo by Brian Vanden Brink, photogra-pher © 2005, Design: Drysdale Associates Interior Designs; (top right) Photo © Tim Street-Porter; (bottom) Photo © Jessie Walker; p. 27: Photo by Brian Vanden Brink, photographer © 2005, Design: Drysdale Associates Inte-rior Designs; p. 28: Photo © Mark Samu, Design: Eileen Kathryn Boyd Interiors; p. 29: (top) Photo © davidduncanlivingston.com; (bottom) Photo by Brian Vanden Brink, photographer © 2005; p. 30: (top) Photo by Andy Engle, © The Taunton Press, Inc.; (bottom) Photo © Steve Vierra/stevevierra-photography.com, Design: Deco-rative Interiors; p. 31: (top) Photo © 2005 Carolyn L. Bates/carolyn-bates.com, Architect: Brad Rabi-nowitz; (bottom) Photo courtesy Harrison Design Associates; p. 32: (left) Photo © Rob Karosis/rob-karosis.com, Design: Diane Hughes; (right) Photo © Tim Street-Porter; p. 33: (top) Photo © Tim Street-Porter; (bottom left) Photo © Steve Vierra/stevevierra-photography.com, Design: Deco-rative Interiors; (bottom right) Photo © Mark Samu, Design: Sherrill Canet Design; p. 34: (top) Photo © Jessie Walker, Design: Kim Elia, Naperville, Il.; (bottom) Photo © davidduncanlivingston.com; p. 35: (top) Photo © Mark Samu, Design: Anne Tarasoff Interiors; (bottom) Photo © Tim Street-Porter; p. 36: (top) Photo © Eric Roth, Design: Weena & Spook; (bottom) Photo © davidduncan-livingston.com; p. 37: (top) Photo courtesy Harrison Design Associa-tes; (bottom) Photo © Steve Vierra/stevevierraphotogra-phy.com, Design: Anthony Catalfano; p. 38: Photo © david-duncanlivingston. com; p. 39: (top) Photo by Brian Vanden Brink, photographer © 2005, Design: Polhemus Savory DaSilva Architects; (bottom) Photo © Tim Street-Porter; p.40: (top) Photo © Eric Roth, Design: Susan Sargent;

(bottom) Photo © davidduncan-livingston.com; p. 41:Harrison Design Associates; p. 42: (top) Photo © Tim Street-Porter; (bottom left & right) Photo © Eric Roth, Design: Susan Sargent; p. 43: Photo © Rob Karosis/ robKarosis.com; p. 44: Photo © Jessie Walker, Design: Lyn & Bill Kavanaugh, Wilmette, Ill.; p. 45: Photos © Eric Roth, (top left) Design: Susan Sar-gent; p. 46: Photo © davidduncan-livingston. com; p. 47: (top) Photo © Tim Street-Porter, Design: Jen-nifer Delonge; (bottom) Photo courtesy Harrison Design Associ-ates; p. 48: Photo © davidduncan-livingston. com; p. 49: (top) Photo © Eric Roth, Design: Gayle Jeney; (bottom) Photo © Tim Street-Porter, Design: Michael Boyd; p. 50: Photo © davidduncanlivingston. com; p. 51: (top left) Photo © Tim Street-Porter, Design: Barbara Barry; (top right) Photo © Tim Street-Porter; (bottom right) Photo © Tim Street-Porter, Archi-tect: Frank Israel; p. 52: (top left) Photo © Tim Street-Porter, Design: Waldo Fernandez; (top right) Photo © Jessie Walker; (bottom) Photo © davidduncanlivingston. com; p. 53: Photo © Jessie Walker; p. 54: Photos © Mark Samu, Design: Lee Najman Interiors; p. 55: (top) Photo © Jessie Walker; (bottom) Photo © Jessie Walker, Design: KAE Berni Interiors, ASID, River Forest.

CHAPTER 3

p. 56: © Steve Vierra/www.steve-vierraphotography.com, Design: Mary McGee; p. 57: (left) Photo © davidduncanlivingston. com; (middle) Photo © Eric Roth, Design: Gregor Cann; (right) Photo © Jessie Walker; p. 58: (top) Photo © Eric Roth, Design: Greg Van Boven; (bottom) Photo © 2005 Carolyn L. Bates/carolynbates.com, Design: Milford Cushman, The Cushman Design Group; p. 59: Photo © Jessie Walker; p. 60: Photo by John Gruen, © The Taunton Press, Inc.; p. 61: Photo © davidduncanlivingston. com; p. 62: © Steve Vierra/www.steve-vierraphotography.com, Design: Anthony Catalfano; p. 63: (left) Photo © Jessie Walker, Design:

Kelly Hutchinson; (right) Photo by Karan Tanaka, © The Taunton Press, Inc.; p. 64: (left) Photo © Jessie Walker; (right) Photo © Tim Street-Porter, Furniture design: Roy McMakin; p. 65: Photo © davidduncanlivingston. com; p. 66: (top) Photo © Mark Samu; (bottom) Photo © Claudio Santini, photographer, Design: Tony Lewis and Marc Schoeplein Architects; p. 67: Photo © david-duncanlivingston. com; p. 68: Photo © Steve Vierra/stevevierra-photography.com, Design: Deco-rative Interiors; p. 69: (left) Photo © Tim Street-Porter; (right) Photo © davidduncanlivingston. com; p. 70: (left) Photo © Eric Roth, Design: Dotty Volpe; (right) Photo © davidduncanlivingston.com; p. 71: Photo by Charles Miller, © The Taunton Press, Inc.; p. 72: Photo © davidduncanliving-ston.com; p. 73: (left) Photo © Eric Roth, Design: Frank Roop; (right) Photo © davidduncanliving-ston.com; p. 74: Brian Vanden Brink, photographer © 2005, Architect: Sally Weston; p. 75: (top) Photo © Jessie Walker; (bottom) Brian Vanden Brink, photographer © 2005, Design: Jeremiah Eck Architects; p. 76: Photo © Eric Roth, Design: Marcus Gleysteen; p. 77: (left) Photo © Eric Roth, Design: Warner Cunningham Achitects; (right) Photo © Mark Samu, Design: Steven Goldgram Design; p. 78: Photo © Steve Vierra/ stevevierraphotography.com, Design: Marion Glasgow; p. 79: (left) Photo © Steve Vierra/steve-vierraphotography.com, Design: Mary McGee; (right) Photo © david-duncanlivingston.com; p. 80: Photo © davidduncanlivingston. com; p. 81: (top) Photo © Mark Samu, Design: Lucianna Samu Design; (bottom) Photo © Claudio Santini, photographer, Design: Tony Lewis and Marc Schoeplein Architects; p. 82: (left) Photo © Steve Vierra/stevevierrapho-tography.com, Design: Kay Flynn Coughlin; (right) Photo courtesy Harrison Design Associates; p. 83: Photo © Mark Samu; p. 84: (left) Photo by John Gruen, © The Taunton Press, Inc.; (right) Photo © davidduncanlivingston.com;

Curtis Henderson; p. 171: (top) Brian Vanden Brink, photographer © 2005, Design: Drysdale Associates Interior Designs; (middle & bottom) Photo © davidduncanlivingston.com; p. 172: (top) (top) Brian Vanden Brink, photographer © 2005, Design: John Morris Architects; (bottom) Photo © Steve Vierra/stevevierraphotography.com, Design: Nancy Fowler; p. 173: Photo © Steve Vierra/stevevierraphotography.com, Design: Eeata Sachon; p. 174: © 2005 Carolyn L. Bates/carolynbates.com, Design: Milford Cushman, The Cushman Design Group; p. 175: (top) Brian Vanden Brink, photographer © 2005, Design: Drysdale Associates Interior Designs; (bottom) Photo © Jessie Walker; p. 176: (left) Photo © davidduncanlivingston.com; (right) Photo © Mark Samu, Design: EJR Architects; p. 177: Photo © Steve Vierra/stevevierraphotography.com, Design: Decorative Interiors; p. 178: (top) Photo © Todd Caverly/ Brian Vanden Brink photos, Design: George Snead, Jr.; (bottom) Brian Vanden Brink, photographer © 2005, Design: Drysdale Associates Interior Designs; p. 179: (top) © 2005 Carolyn L. Bates/carolynbates.com, Design: Milford Cushman, The Cushman Design Group; (bottom) Photo © Steve Vierra/stevevierraphotography.com, Design: Sue Allen; p. 180: Photo © davidduncanlivingston. com; p. 181: (top) Photo © Steve Vierra/stevevierraphotography.com, Design: Mary McGee; (bottom left) Photo © Rob Karosis/robKarosis.com., Design: Dix Shevalier; (bottom right) Photo © Steve Vierra/stevevierraphotography.com, Design: Sue Allen; p. 182: Photo © Steve Vierra/stevevierraphotography.com, Design: Sue Allen; p. 183: (top) Brian Vanden Brink, photographer © 2005, Architect: Sally Weston; (bottom left) Photo © Mark Samu, Design: EJR Architects; (bottom right) Photo © Steve Vierra/stevevierraphotography.com, Design: Nancy Fowler; p. 184: (left) Photo © Jessie Walker; (right) Photo © davidduncanlivingston. com; p. 185: (left) Brian Vanden Brink, photographer © 2005, Design:

Shope Reno Wharton Architects; (right) Photo © Jessie Walker.

CHAPTER 6

p. 186: Photo © Mark Samu, Design: Lucianna Samu Design; p. 187: (left) Photo © davidduncanlivingston. com; (middle) Photo © davidduncanlivingston. com; (right) Photo © Eric Roth; p. 188: Photo © 2005 Carolyn L. Bates/carolynbates.com, Architect: Frederick W. Horton, Tile Design: Lisa Winkler; p. 189: (left) Photo © Mark Samu, Design: Steven Goldgram Design; (right) Photo © davidduncanlivingston. com; p. 190: Photo © Steve Vierra/stevevierraphotography.com, Design: Anthony Catalfano; p. 191: Photo © davidduncanlivingston. com; p. 192: Photo © Mark Samu, Design: Lucianna Samu Design; p. 193: (top left) Photo © davidduncanlivingston.com; (top right) Brian Vanden Brink, photographer © 2005, Design: Dominic Mercadente, Architect; (bottom) Photo © Mark Samu, Design: Custom Designs by Mary and Melissa; p. 194: (left) Photo © Eric Roth, Design: Susan Sargent; (right) Photo © Mark Samu, Design: Lucianna Samu Design; p. 195: (left) Brian Vanden Brink, photographer © 2005; (right) Brian Vanden Brink, photographer © 2005, Design: Drysdale Associates Interior Designs; p. 196: (top) Photo © Jessie Walker (bottom left) Photo © Steve Vierra/stevevierraphotography.com, Design: Robbins Cyr Associates; (bottom right) Photo © Tim Street-Porter; p. 197: Photo © Jessie Walker, Design: Adele Lampert Interiors; p. 198: (left) Photo © Eric Roth, Design: Heidi Pribell; (right) Photo © davidduncanlivingston. com; p. 199: (top) Photo © Mark Samu; (bottom left) Photo © Rob Karosis/robkarosis.com, Design: Denise Rubin, North Sea Interiors; (bottom right) Photo © Roger Turk/Northlight Photography; p. 200: Photo © Steve Vierra/stevevierraphotography.com, Design: Jackie Whalen; p. 201: (top) Photo © Rob Karosis/robkarosis.com, Design: Scott Purceweil, Dovetailed Kitchens; (bottom) Photo © Jessie Walker,

Design: Evalyn Ashmore/ Design Era; p. 202: (top) Photo © davidduncanlivingston.com; (bottom) Photo © 2005 Carolyn L. Bates/carolynbates.com, Design: Geoffrey Wolcott, GKW Working Design; p. 203: (left) Photo © Mark Samu; (right) Photo © Eric Roth; p. 204: (top right) Photo © Roger Turk/Northlight Photography, Design; Chesmore/ Buck Architects; (bottom right) Photo © Rob Karosis/robkarosis.com, Design: The Green Company; p. 205: (top) Photo © davidduncanlivingston.com; (bottom) Photo © 2005 Carolyn L. Bates/carolynbates.com; p. 206: (top) Photo © Roger Turk/Northlight Photography, Design: Carleen Cafferty Interiors; (bottom) Courtesy of Harrison Design Associates; p. 207: (top left) Photo © Steve Vierra; (bottom left) Photo © Jessie Walker; (right) Photo © davidduncanlivingston.com; p. 208: (top)Photo © Tim Street-Porter; (bottom left) Photo © Tim Street-Porter, Design: Tom Callaway; (bottom right) Photo © Rob Karosis/robkarosis. com, Architect: Dix Shevalier; p. 209: Photo © Eric Roth, Design: Connie Driscoll.

CHAPTER 7

p. 210: Photo © Eric Roth, Design: Susan Sargent; p. 211: (left) Photo © Jessie Walker; (middle) Photo © Eric Roth, Design: Susan Sargent; (right) Photo © Jessie Walker; p. 212: Photo © Eric Roth, Design: Susan Sargent; p. 213: Photo © Mark Samu, Design: Anne Tatasoff Interiors; p. 214: Photo © davidduncanlivingston. com; p. 215: (left) Photo © Mark Samu; (right) Brian Vanden Brink, photographer © 2005, Design: George Snead, Jr.; p. 216: Photo © Eric Roth, Design: Gayle Jeney; p. 217: (top) Photo © davidduncanlivingston. com; p. 218: Photo © davidduncanlivingston. com; p. 219: Photo © Eric Roth, Design: Circle Furniture; p. 220: (top left) Photo © Steve Vierra/stevevierraphotography.com; (top right) Photo © Eric Roth; (bottom) Photo © Tim Street-Porter; p. 221: Photo © davidduncanlivingston. com; p.222: (top) Photo © The Taunton Press, Inc.;

(bottom) Photo © Rob Karosis/robkarosis.com; p. 223: Photo © Eric Roth; p. 224: (left) Photo © Jessie Walker; p. 225: (top left) Photo © davidduncanlivingston. com; (top right) Photo © The Taunton Press, Inc.; (bottom) Photo © Wilsonart; p. 226: Photo © Eric Roth, Design: Susan Sargent.; Design: Lucianna Samu Design; (bottom) Photo © davidduncanlivingston.com; p. 228: (left) Photo © davidduncanlivingston.com.; (right) Photo by Charles Bickford, © The Taunton Press, Inc.; p. 229: Photo © davidduncanlivingston. com; p. 230: Photo © davidduncanlivingston. com; p. 231: Photo © Armstrong Flooring; p. 232: (top) Photo © davidduncanlivingston. com; (bottom) Photo © Globus Cork; p. 223: (left) Photo © davidduncanlivingston. com.; (right) Photo © Eric Roth; p. 234: (left) Photo © Jessie Walker; (right) © davidduncanlivingston. com; p. 235: Photo by Karan Tanaka, © The Taunton Press, Inc.; p. 236: Photo © Jessie Walker; p. 237: (left) Photo © Rob Karosis/robkarosis. com, Design: James Coursey, Architect: TMS Architects.; (right) Photo © Eric Roth, Design: Heidi Pribell; p. 238: Photo © davidduncanlivingston. com; p. 239: (left) Photo © The Taunton Press, Inc.; (right) Photo © Steve Vierra/stevevierraphotography.com, Design: Hanry Sauage, Osterville Showhouse; p. 240: Photo © davidduncanlivingston. com; p. 241: (top left) Photo © The Taunton Press, Inc.; (top right) Photo © Jessie Walker; (bottom) Photo by Kevin Ireton, © The Taunton Press, Inc.

CHAPTER 8

p. 242: Photo courtesy Harrison Design Associates; p. 243: (left) Photo © davidduncanlivingston. com; (middle) Photo by Brian Vanden Brink, photographer © 2005, Design: McMillen, Inc. (right) Photo © Steve Vierra/stevevierraphotography.com; Design: Gayle Reynolds; p. 244: (left) Photo © Eric Roth, Design: Laura Glen; (right) Photo © Roger Turk/Northlight Photography, Design: David Weatherford Interiors and

Antiques; p. 245: Photo © Steve Vierra/stevevierraphotography.com, Design: Anthony Catalfano; p. 246: (top left) Photo © Eric Roth; (bottom left) Photo © davidduncanlivingston.com; (right) Photo © Steve Vierra/stevevierraphotography.com, Design: Susan Tutthill; p. 247: Photo © davidduncanlivingston.com; p. 248: Photo © Eric Roth, Design: Weena & Spook; p. 249: (top left) Photo © Eric Roth, Design: Heather Wells; (top right) Photo © Steve Vierra/stevevierraphotography.com, Design: Elfriede Williams; (bottom) Photo © davidduncanlivingston.com; p. 250: (bottom) Photo by Roe A. Osborn, © The Taunton Press; (top) Photo © davidduncanlivingston.com; p. 251: Photo © davidduncanlivingston.com; p. 252: (top) Photo © Steve Vierra/stevevierraphotography.com; Design: Cynthia Clark Interiors; (bottom) Photo © Steve Vierra/stevevierraphotography.com, Design: Decorative Interiors; p. 253: Photo by Brian Vanden Brink, photographer © 2005, Design: McMillen, Inc.; p. 254: Photo © Eric Roth; p. 255: (left) Photo © davidduncanlivingston.com; (right) Photo © Roger Turk/Northlight Photography, Design: Carleen Cafferty Interiors; p. 256: (left) Photo © Jessie Walker; (right) Photo © Eric Roth, Design: Dennis Duffy; p. 257: Photo © Eric Roth; p. 258: (left) Photo by Brian Vanden Brink, photographer © 2005; (right) Photo © Rob Karosis/robkarosis.com, Design: Diane Sovey, Wall to Wall Interiors; p. 259: Photo by Brian Vanden Brink, photographer © 2005, Design: Drysdale Associates Interior Designs; p. 260: (left) Photo © Rob Karosis/robKarosis.com; (right) photo © davidduncanlivingston.com; p. 261: (left) Photo by Kevin Ireton, © The Taunton Press, Inc.; (right) photo ©davidduncanlivingston.com; p. 262: (left) Photo by Brian Vanden Brink, photographer © 2005, Design: Tom Hampson; (right) Photo by Brian Vanden Brink, photographer © 2005, Design: Christina Oliver Interiors; p. 263: (left) Photo by Brian Vanden

Brink, photographer © 2005; (right) Photo by Brian Pontolilo, © The Taunton Press, Inc.; p. 264: Photo © Tim Street-Porter; p. 265: (top) Photos © 2005 Carolyn L. Bates/carolynbates.com, Architect: Tom Koener, Cabinetry: Tom Moore; (bottom) Kevin Ireton, © The Taunton Press, Inc.; p. 266: (top left) Photo © Tim Street-Porter; (bottom left) Photo © Mark Samu, Design: Lucianna Samu Design; (right) Photo by Brian Vanden Brink, photographer © 2005, Architect: Sally Weston; p. 267: Photo by Roe A. Osborn, © The Taunton Press; p. 268: Photo by Steve Vierra/stevevierraphotography.com, Design: Gayle Reynolds; p. 269: (top left) photo by Brian Vanden Brink, photographer © 2005, Architect: John Gillespie; (bottom left) Photo by Steve Vierra/stevevierraphotography.com, Design: Ann Lenox; (right) Photo © Roger Turk/Northlight Photography, Design: Ironwood Builders.

CHAPTER 9

p. 270: Photo © davidduncanlivingston.com; p. 271: (left) Photo © davidduncanlivingston.com; (middle) Photo © Steve Vierra/stevevierraphotography.com, Design: Elisa Fenster; (right) Photo © Tim Street-Porter; p. 272: (left) Photo © Eric Roth, Design: Wolfers Lighting; (right) Photo © davidduncanlivingston.com; p. 273: (left) Photo Brian Vanden Brink, photographer © 2005, Architect: Scott Simons; (right) Photo © Mark Samu; p. 274: Photo © Jessie Walker; p. 275: (top left) Photo © Rob Karosis/robkarosis.com, Architect: Dix Shevalier; (bottom left) photo by Brian Vanden Brink, photographer © 2005, Design: Group 3 Architects; (right) Photo © Steve Vierra/stevevierraphotography.com, Design: Anthony Catalfano; p. 276: Photo © Tim Street-Porter; p. 277: (top left) Photo © Mark Samu, Design: Steven Goldgram Design; (top right) Photo © Claudio Santini, photographer, Design: Arkin-Tilt Architects; (bottom) Photo © Rob Karosis/robkarosis.com, Design: The Green Company; p. 278: (left)

Photo © Tim Street-Porter, Design: Jennifer Delonge; (right) Photo © Eric Roth, Design: Adolfo Perez; p. 279: (top) Photo courtesy Harrison Design Studios; (bottom) Photo © Eric Roth, Design: Dalia Kitchen Design; p. 280: (top) Photo © Steve Vierra/stevevierraphotography.com, Design: Elisa Fenster; (bottom) Photo © Robert Perron, Architect: Elena Kalman; p. 281: Photo by Brian Vanden Brink, photographer © 2005, Architect: Jack Silverio; p. 282: Photo © Mark Samu; Design: KJS Interiors; p. 283: Photo © Mark Samu; p. 284: (left) Photo © Rob Karosis/robKarosis.com, Design: The Green Company; (right) Photo © davidduncanlivingston.com; p. 285: Photo © davidduncanlivingston.com; p. 286: (top) Photo © Steve Vierra/stevevierraphotography.com, Design: Decorative Interiors; (bottom) Photo © Mark Samu; p. 287: (top) Photo ©davidduncanlivingston.com; (bottom) Photo © Steve Vierra/stevevierraphotography.com, Design: Robbins Cyr Assoc.

CHAPTER 10

p. 288: Photo by Brian Vanden Brink, photographer © 2005, Design: Drysdale Associates Interior Designs; p. 289: (left) Photo © davidduncanlivingston.com; (middle) Brian Vanden Brink, photographer © 2005; (right) Photo © Eric Roth, Design: Weena & Spook; p. 290: (left) Photo © Steve Vierra/stevevierraphotography.com, Design: Richard Fitzgerald; (right) Photo by Brian Vanden Brink, photographer © 2005; p. 291: Photo by Brian Vanden Brink, photographer © 2005, Design: Cornelia Covington Smithwick; p. 292: Photo © Mark Samu, Design: Eileen Kathryn Boyd Interiors; p. 293: (left) Photo by Brian Vanden Brink, photographer © 2005, Design: Polhemus Savory Da Silva Architects; (top right) Photo © Claudio Santini, photographer, Design: Linda Applewhite; (bottom right) Photo © Eric Roth; p. 294: Photo © davidduncanlivingston.com; p. 295: (top) Photo © Mark Samu, Location: Vanguard Showhouse; (bottom left) Photo

by Brian Vanden Brink, photographer © 2005; (bottom right) Photo © davidduncanlivingston.com; p. 296: Photo © Jessie Walker; p. 297: (top left) Photo © Jessie Walker; (top right) Photo © Eric Roth; (bottom) Photo © Jessie Walker; p. 298 (bottom left) Photo © Eric Roth, Design: Cindy Seely; (top right) Photo © davidduncanlivingston.com; (bottom right) Photo © davidduncanlivingston.com; p. 299: Photo © davidduncanlivingston.com; p. 300: (left) Photo by Brian Vanden Brink, photographer © 2005; (top right) Photo by Brian Vanden Brink, photographer © 2005, Design: Pete and Paula Stone; (bottom right) Photo © Claudio Santini, photographer, Design: Suyama Peterson Deguch, Architects; p. 301: (left) Photo by Brian Vanden Brink, photographer © 2005, Design: McMillen, Inc.; (top right) Photo © davidduncanlivingston.com; (bottom right) Photo by Brian Vanden Brink, photographer © 2005, Design: Centerbrook Architects; p. 302: (top) Photo by Brian Vanden Brink, photographer © 2005; (bottom) Photo courtesy Harrison Design Associates; p. 303: (top left) Photo by Brian Vanden Brink, photographer © 2005; (bottom left) Photo © Jessie Walker; (right) Photo © Eric Roth; p. 304: Photo © davidduncanlivingston.com; p. 305: (left) Photo © Jessie Walker; (right) Photo © Eric Roth, Design: Weena & Spook; p. 306: (left) Photo © Eric Roth, Design: Brad Morash; (right) Photo © davidduncanlivingston.com; p. 307: (left) Photo © Mark Samu; (right) Photo © davidduncanlivingston.com; Tim Street-Porter; p. 308: (left) Photo © Tim Street-Porter, Design: Hilde Leiaghat; (top right) Photo by Brian Vanden Brink, photographer © 2005, Design: Drysdale Associates Interior Designs; (bottom right) Photo © davidduncanlivingston.com; p. 309: Photo © davidduncanlivingston.com.

For More Great Design Ideas, Look for These and Other Taunton Press Books wherever Books are Sold.

NEW KITCHEN IDEA BOOK
ISBN 1-56158-693-5
Product #070773
$19.95 U.S.
$27.95 Canada

NEW BATHROOM IDEA BOOK
ISBN 1-56158-692-7
Product #070774
$19.95 U.S.
$27.95 Canada

NEW KIDSPACE IDEA BOOK
ISBN 1-56158-694-3
Product #070776
$19.95 U.S.
$27.95 Canada

NEW BUILT-INS IDEA BOOK
ISBN 1-56158-673-0
Product #070755
$19.95 U.S.
$27.95 Canada

TILE IDEA BOOK
ISBN 1-56158-709-5
Product #070785
$19.95 U.S.
$27.95 Canada

TRIM IDEA BOOK
ISBN 1-56158-710-9
Product #070786
$19.95
$27.95 Canada

TAUNTON'S HOME STORAGE IDEA BOOK
ISBN 1-56158-676-5
Product #070758
$19.95 U.S.
$27.95 Canada

TAUNTON'S FAMILY HOME IDEA BOOK
ISBN 1-56158-729-X
Product #070789
$19.95 U.S.
$27.95 Canada

TAUNTON'S HOME WORKSPACE IDEA BOOK
ISBN 1-56158-701-X
Product #070783
$19.95 U.S.
$27.95 Canada

BACKYARD IDEA BOOK
ISBN 1-56158-667-6
Product #070749
$19.95 U.S.
$27.95 Canada

POOL IDEA BOOK
ISBN 1-56158-764-8
Product #070825
$19.95 U.S.
$27.95 Canada

DECK & PATIO IDEA BOOK
ISBN 1-56158-639-0
Product #070718
$19.95 U.S.
$27.95 Canada

TAUNTON'S FRONT YARD IDEA BOOK
ISBN 1-56158-519-X
Product #070621
$19.95 U.S.
$27.95 Canada

For more information visit our website at www.taunton.com.

Ace Books by Jeanne C. Stein

THE BECOMING
BLOOD DRIVE